Family Dysfunction in Tennessee Williams's *The Glass Menagerie*

Other Books in the Social Issues in Literature Series:

Social Issues
in Literature

Family Dysfunction
in Tennessee Williams's
The Glass Menagerie

Dedria Bryfonski, Book Editor

GREENHAVEN PRESS
A part of Gale, Cengage Learning

GALE
CENGAGE Learning·

Detroit • New York • San Francisco • New Haven, Conn • Waterville, Maine • London

Elizabeth Des Chenes, *Director, Publishing Solutions*

© 2013 Greenhaven Press, a part of Gale, Cengage Learning

Gale and Greenhaven Press are registered trademarks used herein under license.

For more information, contact:
Greenhaven Press
27500 Drake Rd.
Farmington Hills, MI 48331-3535
Or you can visit our Internet site at gale.cengage.com

For product information and technology assistance, contact us at

Gale Customer Support, 1-800-877-4253
For permission to use material from this text or product, submit all requests online at www.cengage.com/permissions

Further permissions questions can be emailed to permissionrequest@cengage.com

Articles in Greenhaven Press anthologies are often edited for length to meet page requirements. In addition, original titles of these works are changed to clearly present the main thesis and to explicitly indicate the author's opinion. Every effort is made to ensure that Greenhaven Press accurately reflects the original intent of the authors. Every effort has been made to trace the owners of copyrighted material.

Cover image © Everett Collection/Alamy.

LIBRARY OF CONGRESS CATALOGING-IN-PUBLICATION DATA

Family dysfunction in Tennessee Williams's The glass menagerie / Dedria Bryfonski, book editor.
   p. cm. -- (Social issues in literature)
Includes bibliographical references and index.
   ISBN 978-0-7377-6379-9 (hardcover) -- ISBN 978-0-7377-6380-5 (pbk.)
   1. Williams, Tennessee, 1911-1983. Glass menagerie. 2. Dysfunctional families in literature. 3. Bryfonski, Dedria.
   PS3545.I5365G535 2013
   812'.54--dc23

                                    2012034262

Printed in the United States of America
 1 2 3 4 5   17 16 15 14 13

Contents

Although *The Glass Menagerie* is not strictly autobiographical, there are similarities between the fictional Wingfield family and Tennessee Williams's own family. Both families are dysfunctional, with an alcoholic father, an enabling spouse, a child who develops coping mechanisms, and a child who retreats into her own world.

Tennessee Williams was the son of a boisterous, mostly absent father and a genteel, domineering mother. The family conflict between fragility and brutality that he witnessed as a child became a central theme in his work.

The Glass Menagerie, set during the bleak days of the Great Depression, is Williams's masterly play about family conflict and sibling bonding. Laura and Tom are in conflict with Amanda, who refuses to accept them for who they are. Tom feels a special kinship with Laura but ultimately abandons her.

In *The Glass Menagerie* readers see the dissolution of the Wingfield family through Tom's eyes. Tom's goal was to escape his family and achieve freedom, but once he achieves his goal, he learns he will always be haunted by guilt and memories of his family.

The doomed attempts by Laura and Amanda to escape from their bleak lives mirror the bleak reality of the Great Depression, when the American dream was derailed. Laura and Amanda are seeking a savior, but there is none to be found in Williams's abandoned world.

Although research indicates that most people form deep bonds to even difficult parents, sometimes, for the sake of the adult child, the bond needs to be severed.

Introduction

*T*he *Glass Menagerie* is generally considered to be Tennessee Williams's most autobiographical play. Dakin Williams, the younger brother of Tennessee, has termed the play "a virtually literal rendering of our family life." If that life indeed resembled that of the fictional Wingfields, it is a sad commentary on the Williams family, for the Wingfields are both dysfunctional and doomed. At the end of the play, Amanda realizes that her efforts to secure better lives for her children have backfired and that her hopes for the family's future have been dashed. Tom deserts his mother and sister, cutting off the financial contribution he's able to make to their tenuous existence and dooming himself to a life of relentless guilt. Laura is so traumatized by the rejection of a gentleman caller that she retreats further into a world of fantasy, with any possibility of finding a job or a husband out of the question. It is clear that the household's absent husband and father—"a telephone man who fell in love with long distances"—will play no role in the future of the family. In what ways did the real Williams family resemble this unhappy lot?

The Williams's family heritage is mirrored in *The Glass Menagerie*. Both the Wingfields and Williams came from a gentler, agrarian southern culture to the unfriendly midwestern metropolis of St. Louis. Tennessee's mother, Edwina Dakin Williams, was the daughter of an Episcopal rector, and because her husband, Cornelius, worked as a traveling salesman, Edwina and her children lived with her parents in several small Mississippi towns for the first eight years of Tennessee's life. The Williamses enjoyed social status and what Tennessee termed in his autobiography, *Memoirs*, "the beneficent homelife provided by my beloved Dakin grandparents." This came to a sudden end when Cornelius secured a job as a manager at the International Shoe Company in St. Louis and summoned his family to live with him.

The move to St. Louis put considerable stress on the Williams's marital relations. Edwina found it hard to adjust to life in a grim urban apartment and mourned her loss of social status. A Puritan at heart, she was appalled by her husband's drinking and sexual advances. The Williams's marriage became a battleground. Edwina withheld sex, scolded her husband for his affection for alcohol and loose women, and made Tennessee her unwilling confidant. Similarly, in the play Amanda is unhappy in St. Louis, troubled by her absent husband's drinking problem, is overbearing toward her children, and escapes into her past youth as a southern belle. Williams told friends that Amanda was an "exact replica" of his mother. Perhaps this accounts for the tenderness in his character description:

> "A little woman of great but confused vitality frantically clinging to another time and place. . . . She is not paranoiac, but her life is paranoia. There is much to admire in Amanda, and as much to love and pity as there is to laugh at. Certainly she has endurance and a kind of heroism, and though her foolishness makes her unwittingly cruel at times, there is tenderness in her slight person."

Although the husband in *The Glass Menagerie* is present only through a photograph over the fireplace, his influence is felt throughout the play. The little we know about the husband bears a significant resemblance to Cornelius Williams—both men are absent from home at crucial times and both have a drinking problem. Tennessee was actually far happier before his father reentered his life. His father's first act on meeting him at the train station in St. Louis was to slap him, Tennessee writes in his *Memoirs*:

> "He met us at Union Station. We had scarcely left that curiously designed structure of gray stone, now threatened with

demolition, when we happened to pass an outdoor fruit stand. In passing it, I reached out and plucked a grape. Dad delivered a stinging slap to my hand and boomed out, 'Never let me catch you stealing again!'"

It was an inauspicious beginning, and things only got worse from there. A macho, sometimes violent man, Cornelius had little in common with his sensitive, bookish son. He called Tennessee a sissy and nicknamed him "Miss Nancy." It is little wonder that Williams is quoted by Clive Hirschhorn in the London *Sunday Express* as saying, "When I was younger, I hated him with a passionate loathing. He was a big, powerful man, and he intimidated all of us. . . . My mother hated his guts too." Tensions between father and son would deepen when Cornelius discovers that Tennessee has flunked out of the Reserve Officers Training Corps (ROTC) in his junior year at the University of Missouri. He forced Tennessee to withdraw from college and work at a menial job at the International Shoe Company.

There is one significant difference in the relationship Tennessee Williams had with his parents and the relationship of the Wingfields, however. Tom Wingfield deserts his mother and sister, making their financial situation even more grave. Tennessee Williams, though he left home, later assigned half of the royalties from *The Glass Menagerie* to his mother. With the play's success, she now had the financial resources to divorce his father.

Laura is the most sympathetically drawn character in the play. Due to one leg being shorter than the other, she wears a brace that causes her acute embarrassment. Crippled both physically and emotionally, Laura retreats into a fantasy world where she plays with her glass menagerie figures. Like Tom Wingfield, Tennessee had a sister—Rose—who was mentally fragile and who owned a collection of glass animal figurines. Born only sixteen months apart, the children were inseparable when young, dubbed "The Couple" by family members. In *Conversations with Tennessee Williams,* Tennessee describes their closeness:

> "[Rose] was the member of the family with whom I was most in sympathy and, looking back, her glass menagerie had a meaning for me ... and as I thought about it the glass animals came to represent the fragile, delicate ties that must be broken, that you inevitably break, when you try to fulfill yourself."

However, as she reached adolescence, it became increasingly obvious that Rose was suffering from a mental disorder. She was put into a mental institution in 1937 and lobotomized in 1943. In *The Glass Menagerie,* Tom feels guilty for deserting his sister; Williams was also troubled by guilt because he was not there to prevent his sister's lobotomy.

The similarities between Tom Wingfield and Tennessee Williams are numerous. In addition to sharing a first name (Tennessee's given name was Thomas), both were trapped in menial jobs while they pursued their real passion, writing, at night. Tennessee, like his character Tom, found escape in attending the cinema; however, the most striking parallels are in the family situation. Both have domineering mothers, absent fathers, and a fragile and damaged sister whom they adore but eventually fail.

Tennessee himself made the point that *The Glass Menagerie* is "emotionally autobiographical." The picture he paints of family life mirrors his own experience—that the family unit is not a place of security and love, but rather a battlefield of betrayal and guilt, alienation and despair.

With its lyrical writing, strong characterization, and enduring themes, *The Glass Menagerie* remains one of the most often-produced American plays of all time. The essays that follow explore family dysfunction in *The Glass Menagerie* as well as in twenty-first-century America.

Chronology

1911

Tennessee Williams is born Thomas Lanier Williams on March 26 in Columbus, Mississippi, to Edwina Dakin Williams and Cornelius Williams.

1911–1918

Edwina Williams and her two children live with her parents in the Episcopal parsonages of several southern towns while Cornelius works as a traveling salesman.

1918

The Williams family moves to St. Louis, Missouri, where Cornelius takes a job as branch manager of the International Shoe Company.

1919

Walter Dakin Williams is born to Edwina and Cornelius on February 21.

1929

Williams graduates from University City High School in St. Louis and enrolls at the University of Missouri, Columbia.

1932

Cornelius withdraws Williams from the university following the winter semester and puts him to work at the International Shoe Company warehouse. Williams spends his nights writing.

1935

Williams suffers a breakdown, leaves his job, and recuperates at his grandparents' home in Memphis.

1936

Williams studies at Washington University in St. Louis and continues to write poetry and plays.

1937

After failing to meet Washington University's requirements for graduation, Williams transfers to the University of Iowa where he studies playwriting and production. He has several short plays produced.

1938

Williams graduates with a BA in English from the University of Iowa in August.

1939

Williams lives in several cities, including New Orleans, where he works as a waiter in the French Quarter. He first uses the name "Tennessee" as the author of "The Field of Blue Children," a short story published in *Story Magazine*. In September he meets with Audrey Wood, who becomes his agent.

1940

Williams attends John Gassner's playwriting seminar at the New School for Social Research. In December his play *Battle of Angels* opens in Boston but closes quickly due to poor reviews and a censorship controversy.

1941–1942

Williams lives in a number of cities, holding a variety of jobs. He begins work on the story "Portrait of a Girl in Glass" and the play *The Gentleman Caller*, which will later be developed into *The Glass Menagerie*.

1943

Williams's sister Rose is institutionalized for schizophrenia and undergoes a prefrontal lobotomy. He works briefly as a scriptwriter for Metro-Goldwyn-Mayer.

1944

On December 26 *The Glass Menagerie* premieres in Chicago.

1945

The Glass Menagerie opens on Broadway in March and wins the New York Drama Critics' Circle Award, among other awards.

1947

In December, *A Streetcar Named Desire* opens in New York. The play wins the Pulitzer Prize for Drama and the Donaldson and New York Drama Critics' Circle Awards. Williams meets Frank Merlo, and they become lovers.

1950

The Warner Brothers film version of *The Glass Menagerie* is released.

1951

The film version of *A Streetcar Named Desire* is released.

1952

The film version of *A Streetcar Named Desire* wins the New York Film Critics' Award. Williams is elected to the National Institute of Arts and Letters.

1955

Cat on a Hot Tin Roof opens in March in New York. It wins the Pulitzer Prize for Drama, and the New York Drama Critics' Circle and Donaldson Awards.

1957

Cornelius Williams dies in March. Williams begins psychoanalysis.

1958

The film version of *Cat on a Hot Tin Roof* is released.

1963

Frank Merlo dies of cancer in September. Williams enters a period of depression and drug and alcohol abuse.

1969

In January, Williams converts to Roman Catholicism. Williams enters Barnes Hospital in St. Louis for psychiatric care and withdraws from dependence on drugs and alcohol.

1975

Williams receives the Medal of Honor for Literature from the National Arts Club. His autobiography, *Memoirs*, is published.

1980

In June, Edwina Williams dies. Williams is awarded the Medal of Freedom by President Jimmy Carter.

1983

On February 24 or 25, Williams dies at the Hotel Elysée in New York from choking on a cap from a medicine bottle.

Social Issues in Literature

CHAPTER 1

Background on
Tennessee Williams

The Life of
Tennessee Williams

Thomas P. Adler

Thomas P. Adler is emeritus professor of English at Purdue University and an author of books on American drama.

*Tennessee Williams is generally considered the most important southern dramatist of the twentieth century, according to Adler in the following selection. There are several themes that appear in most of Williams's works, Adler states: the role of illusion in bringing meaning to life, the tension between the agrarian South and the industrial North, the harsh way that society treats its more sensitive members, and the importance of kindness and magnanimity of spirit. The lyrical quality of Williams's dialogue and his empathetic development of female characters distinguish Williams's best works—*The Glass Menagerie, A Streetcar Named Desire, *and* Cat on a Hot Tin Roof*—and make them as relevant today as when they were written, Adler concludes.*

Tennessee Williams is considered by many to be the most important Southern playwright of the twentieth century, and he is arguably second only to Eugene O'Neill among all American dramatists. The conflict between two cultures—an agrarian South, where he was born, that looked back nostalgically to a partly mythical genteel past, and a forward-looking industrialized North that valued pragmatism over beauty, where he moved with his family while still a child—haunted Williams throughout his life and formed one of the enduring tensions in his work. The feeling of displacement, exacerbated later by an awareness of his homosexuality that he felt com-

Thomas P. Adler, "Tennessee Williams," in *Dictionary of Literary Biography, vol. 341: 20th-Century American Dramatists, Fifth Series*, ed. Garrett Eisler. Detroit: Gale, 2008, pp. 276–97. Copyright © 2008 Cengage Learning. All rights reserved. Reproduced by permission.

pelled to keep hidden for much of his playwriting career, gave him a particular compassion for the physically, emotionally, and spiritually vulnerable. That compassion, together with a refusal to pass judgment on others who are in some way different from society's norm, became a distinguishing characteristic of his writing.

In a 1960 essay titled "Tennessee Williams Presents His POV," the playwright succinctly expresses his literary intention: "I dare to suggest ... that the theater has made in our time its greatest artistic advance through the unlocking and lighting up and ventilation of the closets, attics, and basements of human behavior and experience." ...

The Need for Compassion

Williams's abiding thematic motifs [are] the place of illusions and dreams in otherwise thwarted lives; the way socioeconomic conditions and conventional moral norms can constrict human freedom, and the destructive impact of society on its more sensitive members; the imperative to break out of the shell of self and form bonds of human interconnectedness; the necessity to accept human frailty and mortality without despair, or without succumbing to self-indulgent guilt; and, finally, the need for a magnanimity of spirit that allows one to say, along with Williams himself, "There is only one shame—failing a human being who needs you."

Thomas Lanier Williams was born on 26 March 1911, in Columbus; Mississippi, the second of three children of Cornelius Coffin Williams and Edwina Dakin, who were incompatible from the start. Because of tension between his parents, and his father's job as a traveling salesman that included drink and poker and other women, Tom spent his early years living with his mother and older sister Rose in a succession of rectories in Columbus; Nashville, Tennessee; and later in Clarksdale, Mississippi, with his maternal grandfather, Walter, an Episcopal priest, and his grandmother, Rosina. Diphtheria and

Playwright Tennessee Williams in 1945. © Everett Collection Inc/Alamy.

a kidney infection left Tom partially paralyzed for two years, during which he found solace in a world of books; his father later taunted his withdrawn son, nicknaming him "Miss Nancy."

In 1918 the family relocated to St. Louis, where Cornelius got an office job as a branch manager and Tom's younger brother, Dakin, was born. In junior high and high school, Tom began writing Gothic stories, essays, and movie reviews, and he developed a deep friendship with a neighbor girl, Helen Kramer. His first publications came in 1927, with an essay, "Can a Good Wife Be a Good Sport?" in *Smart Set*, and in

1928 with "The Vengeance of Nitocris" in *Weird Tales*. The same year he saw his first Broadway play, the Jerome Kern, and Oscar Hammerstein musical *Show Boat*, and accompanied his grandfather on a European tour. In 1931 Cornelius forced him to withdraw from the University of Missouri at Columbia for failing ROTC [Reserve Officers Training Corps, a military prep program] and took him home to begin working at the International Shoe Company.

While recuperating from a heart problem at his grandparents' home in Memphis in 1935, Williams read and became enthralled with the dramas of Anton Chekhov. He then enrolled at Washington University in St. Louis where he read Hart Crane—who remained a lifetime favorite and provided the epigraphs for many of his plays—and, under the tutelage of the poet Clark Mills Burney, won the top prize in a poetry-writing contest.

Williams undertook his only formal training in playwriting under E.P. Conkle and E.C. Mabie at the University of Iowa, from which he graduated in 1938. Inspired by a newspaper account of the inhumane treatment of rebellious prisoners, Williams wrote the most overtly sociopolitical work of his entire career. However, not until sixty years after it was first written, and fifteen years after the playwright's death, did *Not About Nightingales* (1938) reach Broadway. . . .

Empathy for Society's Misfits

Not About Nightingales introduces many of the motifs that adumbrate the work of the mature Williams: the power of the sustaining dream or illusion; the pervasiveness of human isolation; persecution of the sensitive sexual, racial, or ethnic outsider; the tendency toward cruelty of characters exposed to brutalizing treatment; writing as an expression of repressed feelings; and the necessity of social responsibility and the formation of community. *Not About Nightingales* demonstrates that Williams was never a strictly realistic dramatist, but one always as dependent on the poetry of the theaterical presentation as he was on verbal lyricism.

The year after he graduated from Iowa, Williams settled in New Orleans. where he had his first homosexual affair—though he remained conflicted about his sexuality for some time—and changed his name to "Tennessee" when he entered a collection of one-act plays in a Group Theater contest. There he met Audrey Wood, who became his longtime literary agent. After receiving a $1,000 grant from the Rockefeller Foundation, he enrolled in John Gassner's playwriting seminar at the New School for Social Research in New York, which staged his first works to be seen in the city, including *This Property Is Condemned* (1942). Featuring the teenage girl, Willie, whose life is a poignant mix of sordid reality and romantic imagination as she tries to reimagine her dead sister Alma and her lovers, the short play proposes a retreat into illusion as a protective escape. . . .

Influence of Sister's Mental Illness

During much of the 1940s Williams was on the road, living in Provincetown on Cape Cod, in Taos, New Mexico, and in Key West, Florida; late in the decade he visited Paris, Rome, and London, traveling with Frank Merlo, with whom he began a relationship in 1948 that endured for more than fourteen years. While in Taos, he visited D.H. Lawrence's widow, Frieda. Williams paid tribute to the man whose core belief about pagan naturalism leading to religious transcendence he shared, not only by writing a brief play about his death, *I Rise in Flame, Cried the Phoenix* (produced 14 April 1959), but also by dramatizing a Lawrence short story with Donald Windham in *You Touched Me!*, produced in 1943.

While he was away from St. Louis traveling, or working at odd jobs such as ushering in movie theaters, Williams's beloved sister Rose was subjected in 1943 to a prefrontal lobotomy that doctors thought would cure her of dementia; for the rest of his life, the playwright suffered from guilt over not having been home to prevent its happening. That same year, while under contract as a scriptwriter at M-G-M in Hollywood, Williams wrote "The Gentleman Caller." Revised as *The Glass Menagerie*, it opened in Chicago on 26 December 1944, starring Laurette Taylor, and then went on to Broadway on 31 March 1945, where it ran for 561 performances. The play won the New York Drama Critics' Circle, the Donaldson, and the Sidney Howard Memorial awards.

The episodic action of *The Glass Menagerie* occurs in two time frames: a present time in which a narrator directly addresses the audience, and scenes between these passages of narration that act out the remembered past. This filtering process suggests a mind in conflict with itself, trying to come to terms with choices made earlier, specifically with the guilt that resulted when the narrator decided to pursue his own growth as an individual at the expense of his responsibility to his mother and sister he left behind. The narrative passages also add a sociopolitical dimension to the play, commenting on the Depression, labor unrest in America's large mid-western cities, events in Europe that portend the rise of totalitarian regimes, and the tendency of Americans toward isolationism as they retreat into the world of swing music and sentimental romance, blinding themselves to the conflagration to come. . . .

A Manifesto for Modern Theater

Williams claims that psychologically believable characters are the essence of drama. To make such characters compelling to an audience, he goes beyond employing strictly realistic techniques. In his "Production Notes" to *The Glass Menagerie*— which serve as an important manifesto for the modern theater—Williams expresses his dissatisfaction with any work that depends solely on photographic realism as a means of penetrating to the truth of human experience. Instead, he proposes the need for a transformative, poetic approach, what the narrator in *The Glass Menagerie* calls tricks that create theatrical illusion, making the audience aware they are in a theater watching a play. Rather than straight realism, which Williams terms exhausted, he calls for a "new, plastic theater" that is not language bound but freely incorporates visual and auditory elements—image, color, shape, lighting, music, sound, translucent walls—that help dramatize the characters' subjectivity. In his 1955 essay, "Person-to-Person," Williams names his approach "personal lyricism," a poetic method for letting the characters' inner voice—their "outcry"—be heard more clearly.

That psychological exploration continues in *A Streetcar Named Desire* (1947). . . . The play won Williams his first Pulitzer Prize, as well as the New York Drama Critics' Circle and Donaldson awards, and afforded him the longest Broadway run of his career with 855 performances.

Blanche DuBois is considered by many to be one of the most memorable characters ever created for the American stage; Williams's blend of realistic and expressionistic techniques, including lighting and sound effects that capture the interior condition of Blanche, achieves a depth and subtlety more often found in the novel. *A Streetcar Named Desire* also presents Williams's fullest working out of the myth of the American South and of what happens when the pragmatic intruder from the urban North challenges the values of a society that is uncritically nostalgic about its past. The effects of this tension are apparent in his superbly drawn female characters. Idealized by the men for their purity, and kept dependent economically, they often retreat into a world of illusion. Victims of male domination, they exaggerate normal feminine characteristics, displaying hyper-emotionalism and even sexual seductiveness to compensate for their powerlessness. The play's setting in the raffish French Quarter of New Orleans allows Williams to bring together an ethnically diverse cast of characters, including, along with the declining Southern aristocracy, blacks and Hispanics and descendants of European immigrants, and to raise questions of economic and sexual power. The way that power threatens to destroy sensitivity suggests that what Williams presents in *A Streetcar Named Desire* may be the tragedy of modern civilization as much as that of any single individual. . . .

Although Williams did not publish his longest novel until the mid 1970s and continued to write short stories up until the time of his death, his most successful works of fiction appeared in the late 1940s and early 1950s, with the two collections of short stories, *One Arm and Other Stories* (1948) and *Hard Candy (1954)*, and the lengthy novella, *The Roman Spring of Mrs. Stone* (1950), adapted for the screen in 1961 with Vivien Leigh in the title role. His stories, several of which later served as sources for full-length plays, and which range from the Gothic tale to the bawdy fabliau [a short, comic verse], display the greater freedom in subject matter that Williams enjoyed in this more private medium than was possible in the more public arena of the theater at the time. . . .

Williams Becomes a Public Figure

The mid 1950s began another five-year period during which Williams was as much in the limelight as he had been in the late 1940s, culminating in 1962 when he was the subject of a cover story in *Time* magazine. In *Cat on a Hot Tin Roof* (1955) the Pollitt family has gathered at a plantation in the Mississippi Delta to celebrate Big Daddy's sixty-fifth birthday; but this turns out to be a death day instead, since word has been received (kept secret from Big Daddy) that he is suffering from terminal cancer. So the question becomes which of his two sons will inherit the land. . . .

Cat on a Hot Tin Roof focuses upon suspicion of difference, particularly of sexual difference. Williams's staging emphasizes characters eavesdropping, listening through walls, and making ill-informed accusations that might be far from the truth. Because Williams insists on remaining true to the "mystery" that he sees at the heart of every human personality, he deliberately leaves an aura of ambiguity surrounding Brick's character; this, in turn, has opened him up to criticism for evasiveness and failure to be more explicit about the nature of Brick's sexuality—although the commercial theater of the time placed pressure on Williams to remain circumspect. The play also raises issues of how masculinity should be defined, of how stereotypical definitions, depending on proving oneself through physical prowess, can be broken down, and of how men can develop homosocial bonds among themselves without society (mis)naming them something they are not. Finally, it examines power relationships, both within the institution of marriage and within the larger society. . . .

Drinking, Drugs, and Outing Himself

By the late 1950s Williams had become dependent on artificial stimulants, alcohol and later drugs, as an aid to writing, and after his father died in 1957, he underwent a year of psychoanalysis with the famed Dr. Lawrence Kubie. The death from cancer of his longtime lover, Frank Merlo, in 1963 plunged him deeper into a period of depression that he referred to as his "Stoned Age" and that would continue unabated until the end of the decade. At the beginning of 1969, under pressure from his brother, Williams was baptized as a Roman Catholic at Our Lady Star of the Sea Church in Key West. He ended the year confined for four months to the psychiatric ward at Barnes Hospital in St. Louis.

Reflecting Williams's near crack-up in the late 1960s is *In the Bar of a Tokyo Hotel* (produced 11 May 1969; published 1968). In this work of fractured lines of incomplete dialogue, Williams limns man's fear of mortality and the artist's fear of ineffectuality through a middle-aged wife, Miriam, and her husband, Mark—who may be two sides of one character. . . .

Although the period of his great stage plays appeared to be long over, in the early 1970s Williams enjoyed a certain celebrity, even notoriety, as a public figure in the media. After receiving the Gold Medal For Drama from the National Institute of Arts and Letters, he announced his homosexuality during a television interview with David Frost in 1969, admitting "I cover the waterfront"; this was followed by frank personal interviews appearing in both *Esquire* and *Playboy*. In 1971, he spoke openly against American policy at an anti–Vietnam War rally, the same year that New Directions began publishing the collected plays in eight volumes under the title *The Theatre of Tennessee Williams*. In 1973, the Cathedral of St. John the Divine in New York awarded him its first Centennial Medal; and, as the decade ended, fellow Southerner President Jimmy Carter honored him at the Kennedy Center by presenting him with the Medal of Freedom. . . .

The Off-Broadway production of *Small Craft Warnings* in 1972, which many saw as auguring a possible new beginning for the playwright, was a first for Williams in several ways: he appeared for the first time in one of his plays, hoping thereby to extend its run; and he presented, for the first time onstage in his plays, an unabashedly gay character. Yet, he worried, in the preopening journalistic piece titled "Too Personal," whether by allowing his private life to become so much the "materials" of his drama, he would destroy any claim to universality—even though to not draw upon experience would render the play "a manufactured, a synthetic thing." . . .

Williams's *Memoirs*

Like *The Glass Menagerie*, Williams's *Memoirs* not only play freely with time, moving between the present and the past, they are also fueled by guilt over sexuality and failing others, though presented here in a more undisguised manner. Writing from the perspective of 1972, when he was appearing Off-Broadway as Doc in *Small Craft Warnings* and preparing for the Broadway production of *Out Cry*. Williams recalls his growing up and his bohemian lifestyle during his lengthy apprenticeship as a writer, and talks candidly about his homosexuality, his physical and psychological illnesses, and his heavy dependence on drugs and drink during the 1960s, as well as about the critics' lack of tolerance for his more-experimental plays after *Night of the Iguana*. The presence of his sister Rose dominates these pages, just as her aura is felt in many of his female dramatic characters who suffer from hysteria and retreat into illusion. Williams considered their relationship the strongest "emotional bond" of his life, with her providing the primary example of how to survive extreme suffering with grace. Although these *Memoirs* are not concerned with the dramas that must, Williams believes, speak for themselves, similar thematic motifs recur: the isolation afflicting those who are different from others, devotion to the work of writing, the fear of confinement, the importance of honesty and kindness, the diminishment of creativity with the passage of time, and the need to endure in the face of mortality....

Williams's Best Works Endure

[In 1981] Williams won the prestigious Commonwealth Award; sharing the honor with him was Britain's Harold Pinter, who called Williams "the greatest American playwright." In 1982 Harvard University conferred upon Williams an honorary doctorate.

Sometime late on 24 February or early on 25 February 1983 Williams died in his suite at the Hotel Elysée in New York, apparently from choking on the cap from a medicine bottle. He had wanted to be buried at sea, near the spot where Hart Crane committed suicide, but his brother, Dakin, had the body returned for a funeral mass and burial in St. Louis—a city where Williams had never felt at home. In 1995 the U.S. Postal Service issued a commemorative stamp in Williams's honor.

The works that Williams wrote for the stage after *Night of the Iguana* met with almost universal rejection by audiences and critics alike. Yet, the plays during the last twenty years of his life could not mute the achievement of the first twenty years, with their indelible female characters, their lyrical language, and their painterly command of visual elements. Williams's empathy for all those who are misfits because of their difference—all those whom society names "Other" because of race or class or sexuality—help keep such dramas as *The Glass Menagerie, A Streetcar Named Desire,* and *Cat on a Hot Tin Roof* as contemporary in their appeal to audiences as when they were first written.

The Mental Illness of Williams's Sister Provided Material for His Work

John Strother Clayton

Literary critic and playwright John Strother Clayton is the author of Themes of Tennessee Williams.

A sickly, hypersensitive child who kept to himself during his childhood, Williams formed a deep bond with his sister, Rose, states Clayton in the following article. Rose is the most important person in Williams's life—when she becomes mentally unbalanced during her teens, it has a devastating effect on him, the author maintains. Sister figures are central to the work of Williams, drawn from his own powerful emotional attachment to his own sister, Clayton concludes.

The central element of Williams' past, as he presents it to us in his fiction, is his sister, a sister who became for him the only person in the world who accepted him without reservation, who shared his secret world with him, who loved him, and whom he loved with all the emotional intensity of a deeply sensitive and lonely child. For Williams, as he presents himself in his writing, was both. In his writing it is painfully clear that he lives with his nerve endings raw and exposed, hypersensitively aware of all that impinges upon the senses: sounds, odors, colors, images—only the sense of taste (in the literal meaning of the word) seems to be absent in his vivid awareness of the world about him. To some the "thousand natural shocks that flesh is heir to" [as Shakespeare's Hamlet put it] hardens the metal of their being, tempers the steel;

John Strother Clayton, "The Sister Figure in the Plays of Tennessee Williams," *The Carolina Quarterly*, vol. 12, no. 4, Summer 1960, pp. 47–60. Copyright © 1960 by John Strother Clayton. All rights reserved. Reproduced by permission.

others, experiencing the same or similar traumas, soften so that the slightest pressure leaves its impression for a lifetime. The new boy in every neighborhood in the country is challenged by the local Tom Sawyer, [the title character of Mark Twain's *The Adventures of Tom Sawyer*], or as in [the movie] *Rebel Without a Cause*, forced to prove his manhood in a "chicken run" held by the neighborhood gang. The town hellion who is the minister's son is part of our folklore; the competition between father and son a staple of popular television and screen fare. The ninety-seven pound weakling who, having been bullied on the beach, realizes his fantasies by himself becoming a bully on the beach has produced untold scores of muscle builders with similar ambitions.

Rose Inspired an Early Short Story

Tennessee Williams remained the physically delicate child who did not send away for the barbells, the bullied son who did not fetch Pap a clout alongside the head and escape on a Mississippi raft, the new boy who stayed home when the "chicken-run" was held, and the minister's (grand)son who delayed becoming a hellion until he was old enough to vote.

He stayed at home with his sister. And her love for him and his love for her was the only strength and escape and rebellion that he knew—until he began to write.

The sister appears most clearly in the short *Portrait of a Girl in Glass*, the sketch which was later realized as the poignant memory play, *The Glass Menagerie*, and in the clinically detailed, sensitively written case history of his childhood *The Resemblance Between a Violin Case and a Coffin*, first published in *Flair Magazine* in 1950. In the latter story Williams describes the painful experience of the break-up of the companionship with his sister to which he so desperately clung as a substitute for the other relationships normal to childhood. His situation, evidently, did not go unnoticed by his family. "They were continually asking me why I did not make friends with other children," he writes. "I was ashamed to tell them that other children frightened me...." As for the sister, her "wild imagination and inexhaustible spirit made all other substitute companions seem like the shadows of shades...."

In *The Resemblance Between a Violin Case and a Coffin* we meet most of the elements that will be with us again and again in his work: the seldom present father, "whom I should say, in passage, was a devilish man, possibly not understood but certainly hard to live with," out on the road with his sample case on long trips; the homosexual attachment for the handsome Richard Miles whom "I resented ... fiercely even though I began, almost immediately after learning of his existence, to dream about him as I had formerly dreamed of storybook heroes;" the developing sense of guilt as "I had begun to associate the sensual with the impure, an error that tortured me during and after pubescence;" and the displaced incest-love, "The transference of my interest to Richard now seemed complete. I would barely notice my sister...."

The progression Williams describes is quite clear. He and his sister enjoy a separate world together. His sister reaches puberty, develops mysterious symptoms, and is treated with new gravity and deference by the mother and grandmother. "In this way was instituted the time of estrangement that I could not understand. From that time on the division between us was ever more clearly established." And, as the basis for deep antagonism, "It seemed that my mother and grandmother were approving and conspiring to increase it." Now, almost overnight, his sister's long copper curls are removed, the costume changed, and "I noted ... she had now begun to imitate the walk of grown ladies, the graceful and quick and decorous steps of my mother...."

"For the first time, yes, I saw her beauty. I consciously avowed it to myself, although it seems to me that I turned away from it, averted my look from the pride with which she strolled into the parlor and stood by the mantel mirror to be admired. And it was then, about that time, that I began to find life unsatisfactory as an explanation of itself and was forced to adopt the method of the artist of not explaining but putting the blocks together in some other way that seems more significant to him. Which is a rather fancy way of saying I started writing. . . ."

Desiring His Sister's Suitor

And now, into the scene, comes the young and handsome Richard Miles, carrying his violin case for he is to play in a duet with the sister, who plays the piano. Together, they must rehearse, and, naturally, the sister experiences her first true love. It is a wretched experience, for it turns her into an idiot at the keyboard, forgetting passages of music, making clumsy mistakes, feeling the despair of appearing a fool in the eyes of someone she worships with all the power of adolescence. The best that can be said about the situation is that Richard is kind, helping her through the tough passages, encouraging her when she despairs. To all of this, the young author is a silent and absorbed witness. At first he watches in bitter jealousy this warm relationship with the only person who belongs to him. But as he watches their young and innocent relationship develop, a strange thing happens; he finds himself erotically stimulated by the sight of their rehearsal together. Can it be that Richard is all that he longs to be? Handsome, talented, the love object of his sister? No, of course that is not it. He does not wish to *be* Richard. Such are not his fantasies. Nor does he wish to *love* his sister. That would never do. If he is stimulated by the sight, it cannot be because he loves the sister, it must be because he loves Richard. Of course. And so, "The transference of my interest to Richard now seemed complete. I would barely notice my sister. . . ." Serve her right too. Teach her to desert him!

Is this the answer to the story he tells? Possibly. I do not know. Speculation is inevitable. In any event his fantasy world is now built upon homosexual daydreams involving Richard, and, on one occasion, as he watches a gentle embrace pass between them when his sister has become upset over her repeated failures at the piano, "my body learned, at least three years too early, the fierceness and fire of the will of life to transcend the single body, and so to continue to follow light's curve and time's. . . ." And of course, the feeling of guilt as he says to himself "Yes, Tom, you're a monster!"

In the story *Portrait of a Girl in Glass* we come to know the sister better—the sister as she will appear to us later in *The Glass Menagerie* and as her ghost will appear in many other ladies to come. Here the locale is part of the new and difficult period of Williams' life, when his family had moved to St. Louis where he was to experience the horror of "a small wage earner in a hopelessly routine job," where he was to learn what it meant to be among the have-nots and so regarded, and where he was to live amid bleak surroundings, watching the slow deterioration of his sister which was eventually to lead her to a mental institution. It is here in this drab depression home that we first meet "Laura," who "made no positive motion toward the world but stood at the edge of the water, so to speak, with feet that anticipated too much cold to move."

It is in this story that Williams gives us an early glimpse of his great talent for effectively utilizing concrete surroundings for both their dramatic and symbolic value. The alley below the sister's room is called Death Valley because in it cats are trapped by a "particularly vicious dirty white Chow who stalked them continually." From this world, Laura retreats. "The areaway had grown to be hateful to Laura because she could not look out on it without recalling the screams and the snarls of killing. She kept the shades drawn down, and . . . her days were spent almost in perpetual twilight." Within this setting, Williams evokes a memorable image, "The charm of the room was produced by his sister's collection of glass. . . . When you entered the room there was always this soft, transparent radiance in it which came from the glass absorbing whatever faint light came through the shades on Death Valley."

The girl who had been his alter ego as a child, whose fingers had stumbled over the keys in the presence of a handsome lad, is now too shy and withdrawn to face the world. To her, Williams gives three avenues of escape from reality: her animals, her records, and a book.

The animals provide her with a fantasy world and fantasy companionship; the records take her back into, the past. "Laura seldom cared for these new records, maybe because they reminded her too much of the noisy tragedies in Death Valley or the speed-drills at the business college. The tunes she loved were the ones she had always heard." From the book, *Freckles*, by Gene Stratton Porter, Laura is provided with a "phantom lover." According to Williams, Freckles, "a one-armed orphan youth who worked in a lumber-camp, was someone that she invited into her bedroom now and then for a friendly visit. . . ." These avenues—the past, fantasy, the phantom lover—will all appear again.

The Laura of *Portrait of a Girl in Glass* is essentially the same person when she reappears in *The Glass Menagerie*, though she has been deprived of her phantom lover. She has been compensated for this loss, however, by the addition of a physical flaw—a device that Williams will utilize frequently throughout his work—both to represent and to account for the flawed nature of her character. It is an outward and visible sign of an inward and spiritual flaw.

The Sister Deserts the Brother

When we next see the sister, a considerable change has taken place; though the family group remains the same: mother, sister, brother, and absent father. They appear in another of Williams' memory plays, *The Long Goodbye*, which deals with a young Depression writer during the early days of the [Franklin D.] Roosevelt administration. He alone remains in the apartment once occupied by his family, and he, too, is moving on. As workmen remove the contents of the apartment various elements evoke memories from the past, some of which are dramatized while others are narrated. The theme of the play is stated in a conversation between brother, Joe, and a companion, Silva:

SILVA: Goodbye? 'S not in my vocabulary! Hello's the word nowadays.

JOE: You're kidding yourself. You're saying goodbye all the time, every minute you live. Because that's what life is, just a long, long goodbye! To one thing after another! Till you get to the last one, Silva, and that's—goodbye to yourself!

During the "flashbacks" we see the gradual estrangement between Joe and his sister, Myra. Joe is jealous and suspicious of the girl's suitors, accuses her of cheap conduct, and triumphantly confronts her with the evidence of premeditation—a contraceptive—dropped by one of her callers. (A dramatic device, incidentally, which was to be repeated in *The Rose Tattoo*, to the scandalized view of drama critic Robert Coleman who professed to be "revolted.") That Joe is more than justified in his suspicions is possible, indeed probable, as Myra infinitely prefers the escape she has chosen to the deadly, poverty-ridden life of a shop girl. So the sister who goes out with other men disappears from his life, looking like a whore—"like a cheap one, Myra, one he could get for six!" And the brother is left alone.

Of course another kind of ending to the story is possible. The sister need not desert the brother. Indeed if one may dream—and why not?—the brother can possess the sister. It is a dangerous thought, a guilty thought, a thought that should be hidden. But it is a consummation devoutly to be wished by the brother figure in Williams' works. . . .

The Object of Desire

The progression of the sister figure in the works of Tennessee Williams is clear. A montage of his short stories and plays would present her as a child desired by the brother. She is a delicate and shy creature, and the brother figure experiences a great deal of guilt because of his desire for her. Though he may experience fantasies in which a relationship between them is realized in their youth, maturity brings estrangement. Eventually the sister is degraded and destroyed. Williams' characters will continue to show an attraction for the child-woman, and his mature women will continue to be portrayed as promiscuous and degraded or (in the case of the mother figure) dominant vampires who drain the man of vitality as they seek to subject him to their own will and purpose. The sister figure derives her importance from her family relationships. When divorced from the family, she becomes another familiar Williams' figure, The Delicate Lady. Deprived of the security offered by either family or marriage, she will turn to fantasy, promiscuity, and madness, as we see her in Blanche Du Bois in *A Streetcar Named Desire*, or Mrs. Harwicke-Moore in *The Lady of Larkspur Lotion*, or Edith Jelkes in *The Night of the Iguana*, or Miss Collins in *Portrait of a Madonna*. It is almost as though some ritual revenge were taking place as the woman who dares to leave childhood must be driven to the asylum or branded as a whore.

Williams Displayed Imaginative Talents as a Child

Dakin Williams, as told to Robert Bray

An attorney, politician, and author, Dakin Williams was the younger brother of Tennessee Williams. He died in 2008. Robert Bray is the founding editor of the Tennessee Williams Annual Review *and a professor of English at Middle Tennessee State University.*

Although the relationship between Tennessee and Dakin Williams was often stormy, Dakin provided considerable support to his brother during his life and is credited with preserving his legacy following his death, Robert Bray states in the following interview. Dakin suggests that a major source of conflict between the two brothers was Tennessee's sexual orientation. Another episode of conflict occurred when Dakin had his brother committed to a psychiatric hospital, Dakin relates. Dakin considers his brother's greatest talent as a dramatist to be his lyricism.

Dakin Williams, born eight years after Tennessee, has come to regard himself as a "professional brother." Having retired in large part from his law practice, Mr. Williams now spends a considerable portion of his time helping perpetuate the memory of his brother. Whenever Dakin Williams appears at literary festivals or at productions of his brother's plays, he is courted by the press and responds to inquiries about Tennessee with good humor and candor. While it may be true that Mr. Williams does not eschew the spotlight and has cultivated an image of the accomplished eccentric, this persona should not obscure his keen intellect, his generosity, and his

Dakin Williams, interviewed by Robert Bray, "An Interview with Dakin Williams," *The Mississippi Quarterly*, vol. 48, no. 8, Fall 1995, p. 776. Copyright © 1995 by The Mississippi Quarterly. All rights reserved. Reproduced by permission.

dedication to promoting his brother's work. Dakin Williams is the author of the *Bar Bizarre* and co-author of *Tennessee Williams: An Intimate Biography*. He knows all of his brother's plays very well and can recite many of the characters' lines from memory.

Despite their sometimes tempestuous relationship, Dakin Williams provided tremendous support for his brother during Tennessee's drug-hazy decades and doubtless saved his brother's life during the commitment to Barnes Hospital in 1969. Although this commitment and the St. Louis burial have subjected Dakin Williams to public remonstration, in this interview Dakin reveals his side of the story. The interview took place over drinks at Williams's home, in Collinsville, Illinois, where he and his wife, Joyce, have lived for years. It began on the evening of May 18, [1995,] and concluded over breakfast the next morning. I started by asking Williams to recall some of his nascent memories of his older brother and to provide insights into Tennessee Williams's personality from the perspective of someone uniquely qualified to do so.

Memories of Early Life

Robert Bray: What are some of your earliest memories of your brother?

Dakin Williams: Naturally, no one has any good memories before five or six years old, and my memory would be after that, when my brother would entertain me by telling stories. He had a fantastic imagination, and we would sit down, and he would make up quite fantastic stories, and I would enjoy them. Early on, my brother resented the fact that my father loved me and disliked him—called him "Miss Nancy." So there was sort of a sibling rivalry . . . early, my brother was jealous of me because my father would pick me up and hold me. In my brother's letters from Clarksdale he would write to my sister, Rose, when he was about ten and I was about two, and say he was coming home soon. He'd write, "Kick King Dakin off his throne."

Tell me something about your early years in St. Louis, the setting for The Glass Menagerie.

We lived on Westminister, the only apartment building in a very fashionable area. All the other places were nice Victorian homes. There was a class distinction in St. Louis that our family was unaccustomed to because it was based on money.

Did Tennessee sense this disparity between the social classes? How difficult was the adjustment for a young boy?

He was made to feel awkward, because when he was at public school suffering from diphtheria, he wasn't able to participate in sports. When he would sit on the curb by the playground, as the other boys ran by they would kick him and persecute him because he had a Southern accent and gave the appearance of being a sissy....

Family Resemblances

Could you describe some of the actual similarities between Amanda and Miss Edwina and Laura and Rose?

My mother was the "spitting image" of Amanda, so much so that my brother, after he became a success, felt obligated to give her fifty percent of the profits of the play. My sister, of course, had psychological handicaps but was not crippled. My sister, at least according to my brother, was really more talented than he was.

What happened, in fact, to Rose's glass menagerie?

Well, it wasn't much of a menagerie—just two or three pieces on a little glass ledge in her bedroom. They were probably thrown out in the move—very cheap little things, probably purchased at Woolworth's.

Your family moved around a great deal in St. Louis during your early years. How did these moves affect the family?

Well, the first move I remember from Westminister was to 5 South Taylor. I have very good memories of that complex. The Westminister apartment had no fire escape.

So in other words, Tennessee probably had both places in mind as the setting for The Glass Menagerie?

Yes, although neither place was as shabby as portrayed in the play.

In the play, the father, Mr. Wingfield, appears only in a photograph. Was your father away often?

No, and that was one of the major problems of our family. When we lived in Mississippi, we lived with my grandfather, the Reverend Dakin, and my father was never at home except for once or twice on weekends. When we moved to St. Louis, my father was home all the time, and he was a very difficult person, especially in regard to sex. My mother thought sex was very dirty, and my father was eager to get it as much as he could, wherever he could get it. . . .

Writing Habits

Before Tennessee went off to college, did you ever see him keeping a notebook?

Yes, he wrote constantly. First of all, after he was taken out of Missouri University, my father put him to work at International Shoe Company, and it was there that my brother developed a hatred for the factory and for St. Louis. When he came home at night he would read and write until four in the morning. He had a compulsion to write, and every time he finished something he'd rush to the post office and send it out, and then every week he'd get a whole flock of rejection notices of his short stories and poems.

What do you know of his work habits? They are fairly well documented, but did he really write every day?

Yes, he did. He maintained a regimen of writing when he was successful. Before that, he wrote after work.

During the good and bad times, during his professional hills and valleys, did he correspond with the family?

Yes. He kept in constant touch with us, particularly with my mother.

Tennessee Williams in 1969, the year his brother Dakin committed him to a mental institution. © AP Images.

What was the first opening you went to? How would you characterize these openings? Were they festive affairs?

A matter of intense anxiety, because opening night was, of course, very critical to his success. Tennessee, Audrey Wood [his agent], my mother and I, along with others, would all wait at a restaurant. They'd bring in great food, but nobody could eat until the reviews came in. The reviews were read at the table.

Southern Identity

Even though your brother lived outside of the South for most of his life, he has said in interviews that he regarded himself as a Southerner. Why do you think he retained this sense of Southern identity?

Well, my brother spent every summer down at Clarksdale with my grandparents, so there were eight or ten years when he was there all summer.

So you think that his being in the Mississippi Delta summer after summer allowed him to absorb the material that later went into his plays?

Yes, because he was always listening to those stories. He had big ears, and that's what people did—they didn't have television or radio—they sat on verandas and told stories. And later on he lived in Memphis, where my grandfather retired, to recover from his breakdown from working at International Shoe Company.

Do you think he held romantic views of the South?

I do. Not realistic, but romantic recollections, like those of Blanche [DuBois of *A Streetcar Named Desire*] and Amanda.

Besides [Anton] Chekhov, [D.H.] Lawrence, and [Stephen] Crane, can you think of any other early literary influences on your brother?

Well, he read extensively and wrote every night until four a.m. My mother would wake him up at six, to go to work, and this is what caused his nervous breakdown. . . .

Sources of Conflict

In terms of your relationship with your brother in your more mature years, some of your misunderstandings have been widely documented. But when you had these misunderstandings, did you attempt to discuss openly your differences?

Yes, but he usually got furious with me. He usually considered me judgmental about things such as his sexual preference. He was very, very touchy, and I was always on the defensive. But I constantly tried to cheer him up about things to which he was sensitive, such as the Catholic Church's damnation of his movie *Baby Doll*. I told him one time during dinner in Miami that the Catholic Church wasn't all bad. I said to him, "You know, Tom, that there is a Jesuit Priest that teaches at Regis College in Denver. Your plays are compulsory reading in his drama course." And Tom said, "Oh, wonderful! What's the professor's name?" I said, "They call him 'Dirty Books Boyle.'" Oh, he was furious.

Of course, one major misunderstanding occurred when you had your brother committed to Barnes Hospital. Why don't you tell your side of the story?

Well, it was necessary, and by now nearly everybody knows it. When I first put Tennessee in there, I tricked him because I knew from Audrey Wood's reports that he was in a very desperate condition. He called me up and asked me to come to Key West. He said, "Dakin, an attempt will be made on my life tonight." I said, "Well, Tom, I can't come tonight (it was about 9:00 p.m.), but I can come tomorrow. Is this OK?" He said, "Oh, yes, do come." He had burned himself badly with coffee because he couldn't walk three feet without falling flat on his face. So I decided to get him on the plane to St. Louis. We had trouble in Nashville because they stopped serving him on the plane after two drinks. It was Sunday, and we couldn't get any booze, which made him furious. In St. Louis, I took him to my mother's house. I had booze there, and that pacified him. Since I had to work the next day, I had arranged for an ambulance to take him to Barnes Hospital, but he refused to go. So around noon he was feeling so bad that he took a taxi with my mother to the hospital. I arranged to get him the most expensive room in the "Queenie" Tower. It had a big swimming pool and skylights. He was very pleased, lying up in bed with a blue stocking cap on, with his blue bag full of pills next to his bed. It was full of seconal, speed, everything imaginable from Dr. Feelgood Jacobs [Max Jacobson, who administered drugs to celebrity clients].

He was great until that night, when the doctors said that he was dying from acute drug poisoning. Then when his bag was confiscated, he got out of bed, threw on some pants, and called a taxi to Lambert Field so he could fly to New York. "I'm going to finish my recovery at the Plaza Hotel," he said. And so I had to do something. I called a cousin of mine who's on the staff of Barnes, and he told me I could keep him in by force for ten days, at the end of which time he could demand to be released. We were going back upstairs to his room, when a friend of mine, Robert Ortega, a well-known photographer, wanted to meet him. I told him that this was not the time or place, but he insisted. He put an arm around Tom's shoulder in the hospital. Tom looked at him very coldly and said, "Who are you?" Ortega said, "Oh, I'm a friend of your brother Dakin." Tom coldly looked at him and said, "Well, I wouldn't brag about that!" When Ortega left, an intern told Tom to sit down in a wheel chair; then he injected him, and he passed out in a few seconds. He woke up the next morning in this whitewashed room, with bars on the windows, the only place I could keep him from walking out of. When he woke up he was disoriented. He couldn't believe what he was seeing. He said, "Where am I—at the Plaza?"

So how long was he committed?

Well, he could have walked out in ten days, but he didn't know that. And I wasn't about to tell him his rights, even if I am a lawyer. The doctors didn't either. He had four convulsions from drug withdrawals and blamed me. He kept asking when he could leave for three months, as the drugs gradually left his system. The doctors told him, "As soon as Dakin says so." He seethed with rage until I arrived one night, and then attacked me. He would ask me, "When can I get out of here?"

And I would say to him, "When the doctors say you can." So he finally saw that he should at least pretend to be cooperative. So I would come to see him at night, and we'd play bridge, and he'd paint during the day. He didn't write, except to [director Elia] Kazan and others, asking them to get him out. His mail was opened and checked before he could read it, and this made him furious. He left when he was cured, and I brought him home.

After the hospital experience, did he continue to use drugs?

No, he stayed off them because of that experience. This was in January of 1970, and he knew that in order to write he had to stay off drugs. He was perfect for about five years, until a young man who moved in with him at Key West got him started on some of them again.

In your estimation, how did these drugs affect his writing?

He no longer wrote objective characters. Every play he wrote on drugs was a dramatic self-portrait; they always concerned two people, like the brother and sister in *Out Cry*, a wonderful play. *In the Bar of a Tokyo Hotel* both characters are sides of himself.

Do you think Out Cry *is about Tennessee and Rose?*

No, it's about him and himself. Of course, Rose would be somewhat in his mind also. . . .

What do you consider your brother's greatest legacy as a dramatist?

His poetic ability, which set him apart. [Playwright Eugene] O'Neill had power, but Tom had poetry.

Social Issues in Literature

CHAPTER 2

The Glass Menagerie and Family Dysfunction

There Are Similarities Between the Dysfunctional Williams and Wingfield Families

Gilbert Debusscher

Gilbert Debusscher is on the faculty of humanities at the Université Libre de Bruxelles in Belgium. He has published extensively on such contemporary dramatists as Edward Albee, Jack Richardson, Willy Russell, Tennessee Williams, Harold Pinter, Arthur Miller, and Edward Bond.

In The Glass Menagerie *Williams vividly portrays the dynamics of a family made dysfunctional because of the alcoholism of the father—a family situation that mirrored his own, Debusscher suggests in the following selection. The typical reaction of a dysfunctional family to alcoholism is denial, and family members become enablers, he explains, a pattern followed in both the Williams and Wingfield families.* The Glass Menagerie *is Williams's most autobiographical play because in it he reflects the dysfunction of his own family as well as touching on his own sexual orientation, Debusscher concludes.*

Alcoholism is a disease that affects not only the victim but the whole family as well. Therapists and psychologists have known for a long time that attention must be paid to the entire family in an effort to break the patterns of dysfunction established by years of alcoholic behavior. In dysfunctional families, regardless of whether the cause is alcohol or not, emotions are repressed and twisted; they are either not shared or manipulated in a judgmental, blaming fashion. Dysfunc-

Gilbert Debusscher, "Tennessee Williams's Dramatic Charade: Secrets and Lies in *The Glass Menagerie*," *The Tennessee Williams Annual Review*, vol. 3, 2000, pp. 1–27.

tional families share certain common traits such as attitudes of rigidity, reverence for past traditions to the detriment of the present, insistence on roles and rituals. For a while these were diagnosed as the cause of alcoholism; instead, it is now believed that these are coping techniques that a family adopts to maintain a certain degree of cohesion and integrity and to create a semblance of sanity. The common denominator of the alcoholic, the spouse, and the children is denial: the unwritten law of the alcoholic home is that there is no problem. There is a symptomatic avoidance of the truth. A network of lies binds the family together. Making excuses, avoiding truth, and creating fantasies become a way of life, extending beyond the original cause—the alcoholism—and invading all other issues.

Amanda Is a Classic Enabler

In *Menagerie* Williams draws indirect attention to Mr. Wingfield's alcoholism in the two or three instances . . . when Amanda reveals her deep-seated fears that Tom might become a drinker or that Mr. O'Connor may already be one, thus indicating that she is well aware that alcoholism is a pattern of family behavior that tends to be repeated by successive generations either through direct filiation, the son taking over his father's drinking habits, or through alliance, the daughter marrying an alcoholic, as did her mother. The original alcoholic, Mr. Wingfield, has abandoned the family a long time ago—probably sixteen years before, in fact—and therefore for much longer than the real-life model. Miss Edwina and Cornelius [Williams] separated only after the royalties of *Menagerie* had made Edwina financially independent, but the disappearance of an alcoholic from the family circle does not reduce, any more so than his treatment or possible recovery, the problems experienced by the spouse and children. Their behavioral scripts are internalized, so their roles are perpetuated.

Amanda still possesses the characteristics of the enabler. She fails to see her situation with objectivity. She is afraid of abandonment and engages in destructive rituals, primarily neurotic nagging. In so doing, she displays the urge to control that is so common to the enabling spouse. It is as if she had a surplus of willpower to compensate for the lack of it in the drinker. Like Maggie, in *Cat [on a Hot Tin Roof]*, the co-dependent becomes addicted to the need to control and bears the joyless burden of it. Thus, Amanda is unwilling to allow her children to become adults. She is presumptuous, demanding, and insensitive. She blinds herself to Laura's real physical condition: "Laura, I've told you never, never to use that word!" As she pushes Laura towards Jim, it is clear she has never paused to find out who her daughter really is, nor what her aspirations might be, nor has she ever considered modes of living other than her own. Along the same destructive line, she insists that Tom remain the family's beast of burden: "What right have you got to jeopardize your job? Jeopardize the security of us all?" He is the breadwinner, but she assumes the right to censor his reading material as if he were a child!

Amanda is possessed by the overwhelming fear that Tom will follow in his father's footsteps. To Tom, she desperately says, "When I see you taking after his ways! Staying out late—and—well, you had been drinking the night you were in that—terrifying condition!" The specter of Mr. Wingfield's unmentioned alcoholism is as constantly present as his laughing photograph. Voiced regularly, her fear is, ironically, what contributes to drive Tom away. Those who study alcoholic families have found that the children's behavior falls into predictable categories. Although these roles are clear, children can play more than one. In the Wingfield family, Laura is the lost child, and Tom is the responsible one. Typically, in response to the distress in the family, these children, to survive, had to develop coping behaviors. Laura withdraws into a world of her own. Fearful of relationships, painfully shy, feeling inadequate

In The Glass Menagerie, *Amanda struggles with the effects of her husband's alcoholism on herself and her family. Here, actress Jessica Lange portrays Amanda in a 2007 production of the play.* © Geraint Lewis/Alamy.

and rejected, she would prefer to walk around Forest Park every day rather than face sure mortification at Rubicam's Business College. Jim's observation is correct: she does have an inferiority complex, a common situation for children growing up in alcoholic homes. Her refuge is to escape from reality.

Fantasy and Guilt

Children use fantasy to survive chaos and pain. Children in dysfunctional homes frequently invent "a private world that gives them a way to escape from time to time so they can keep from being pulled into the craziness" [according to Judith Seixas and Geraldine Toucha in *Children of Alcoholism*]. The make-believe world becomes a sanctuary. Laura is happy spending hours playing with her menagerie, identifying with the unicorn, or listening to her scratchy records. Often such a child ultimately finds refuge, as an adolescent, in alcohol. Laura has not found that avenue. But Tom has. The responsible child, Tom is supporting the family. But, as he combines roles, our "Shakespeare" lives in a nether world of poetry and escape, alcohol and dreams of the merchant marine. Amanda's accusation is quite accurate: "You live in a dream; you manufacture illusions!" This is a common family trait. No one confronts reality, because it is so painful.

Children of alcoholics are heavily burdened by the responsibility of parenting, which usually falls on the older children. Although in this case the younger child, Tom, being the resident male and not physically handicapped, has shouldered this burden. He feels responsible, yet trapped and deeply resentful; and he feels guilty for his reaction. A common rule in the alcoholic home is "Don't be selfish". To preserve the dysfunctional system, it is essential that he not address his own needs but sacrifice himself for the family. Failure to do so is punishable by eternal guilt. These messages are sent repeatedly by Amanda. When she senses his urge to flee from her smothering control, she delivers an ultimatum to Tom:

Amanda: I mean that as soon as Laura has got somebody to take care of her, married, a home of her own, independent—why, then you'll be free to go wherever you please; on land, on sea, whichever way the wind blows you! But until that time you've got to look out for your sister. I don't say we because I'm old and don't matter! I say for your sister because she's young and dependent.

The final interchange between Tom and his mother illustrates the fatal feature of the controlling parent:

Amanda: Don't think about us, a mother deserted, an unmarried sister who's crippled and has no job! Don't let anything interfere with your selfish pleasure! Just go, go, go—to the movies!

Tom: All right, I will! The more you shout about my selfishness to me the quicker I'll go, and I won't go to the movies!

Amanda: Go, then! Go to the moon—you selfish dreamer!

In his farewell address to the audience, Tom confesses that his mother's imposition of guilt was effective. To this day he thinks with regret of how he left Laura: "Oh, Laura, Laura, I tried to leave you behind, but I am more faithful than I intended to be!"

Permanent scars are inflicted on the child in such a warped home. There is a lack of emotional bonding between parent and child. The stress even on the non-alcoholic parent is so severe that nothing is left for the child. This lack of emotional support is perceived by the child as rejection. Adding to this condition, the negative emotions—anger, resentment, blaming, guilt—are so dominant and so painful in the dysfunctional family that attempts are made by all to become nonfeeling. Thus healthy relationships are denied or postponed; the children are emotional cripples. . . . One research group recognizes a problem of sexual identity in the offspring of alcoholic parents. The inability to express emotions, the lack of love, and the absence of bonding with an appropriate gender role model combine to create a propensity towards homosexuality. Tom clearly falls into this category. Amanda even tells Tom she does not want him to take after his father, except for one crucial feature: "The care he always took of his appearance. He never allowed himself to look untidy". This is not surprising. Appearances are very important in the distorted world of the alcoholic family.

Recognizing the role of the dysfunctional family in *Menagerie* provides a fuller understanding of the dynamics of the play. Williams's sensitivity and understanding in using these models of typical alcoholic behavior correspond to the findings of many of those who do professional work in the field of alcohol abuse: most of them, as did Williams, grew up in alcoholic homes themselves. Williams's play reveals the dynamics of alcoholism and its impact on the family unit as clearly as, although more poetically than, the clinical case studies in the abnormal psychology textbooks. Conversely, understanding the alcoholic pattern can enable us to understand Williams with new insight.

Just as Amanda's "spine" is the need for security provoked at least as much by her having married an alcoholic as by the socio-economic circumstances of the late Thirties, Tom's may be viewed as the need to hide his homosexuality from Laura, Amanda, and Jim—and control the inner revolt which is the symptom of it. Williams seems to have been a sexual late bloomer; and his sexuality was, for a while at least, not clearly focused, but by the time he came to write the early drafts of *The Glass Menagerie* he had acknowledged, at least to himself, his homoerotic preference. . . .

Williams Hints at Homosexuality

It is surprising how little attention has been paid until recently to the sexual orientation of Tom Wingfield, the author's alter ego in the play. . . .

Tom's refusal to abide by the meal rituals, and his reluc-
tance to listen to the family saga reveal a rebelliousness, a refusal to conform, to pretend to be and act like the others, to
suppress that otherness which nature has planted in him. His
restlessness, his impatience, his swearwords, his outbursts, his
drinking, and his final flight may all be symptoms of the
bottled up frustrations of the gay person in the straight-laced
environment created and insisted on by Amanda. His sarcasm
is aimed at the modes of courtship and marital arrangements
of the heterosexual world. It is surely not an accident that
having heard the "seventeen gentlemen callers" story many
times ("Again?"), Tom would interrupt to ask a question about
the widow of the brilliant Fitzhugh boy with the full knowledge that he is the one who never married. Amanda's enam-
ored tirade about him and her regrets about a romance that
never materialized adumbrate Blanche's relationship with the
enigmatic Allan Gray [in *A Streetcar Named Desire*], which did
materialize with tragic consequences. Tom's irony towards the
bygone world of Blue Mountain is tinged with fear or diffi-
dence when it comes to the present, in particular the world of
the warehouse. Tom is a solitary figure in the workplace—
where his favorite spot is a "cabinet of the washroom"; where
people talk behind his back—Jim tells him "Mr. Mendoza was
speaking to me about you"—and where they call him names—
"Shakespeare" is not a charitable nickname for an aspiring
poet. He remains separate from his workmates who regard
him first "with suspicious hostility" and later with "a smile
(provoked by) an oddly fashioned dog who trots across their
path at some distance". Is it stretching credibility too far to
read the reactions of the warehouse people as a result of the
stereotypical perception of the "other" and the "different"?
The nature of that "otherness" in the early 1940s had to be
presented on the surface as a poetic disposition at odds with
the industrial surroundings, but homosexuality may be an

equally plausible ground—and moreover not exclusive of the other—to explain suspicion, hostility, aloofness, and estrangement.

In this alienating milieu Tom does not know anything about anybody. When faced with his mother's reproach concerning his ignorance about Jim's marital plans, he counters that "The warehouse is where I work, not where I know things about people". This is as much as to say that there is an unspoken code concerning privacy which he approves of, with the understanding that it also protects him against the unwelcome inquisitiveness of others about *his* marital plans. . . .

His Most Autobiographical Play

The Glass Menagerie is Williams's most autobiographical play and, paradoxically, as we get to know the playwright's life more fully, we also come to see its dramatic mirroring deepen. In other words, the painting reveals hitherto hidden shades that confirm the artist's honesty and integrity.

The Glass Menagerie Depicts the Tension Between Gentle Illusion and Harsh Reality

Signi Falk

A professor, literary critic, short-story writer, and director, Signi Falk taught English for twenty-four years at Coe College in Cedar Rapids, Iowa.

Tennessee Williams is noted for his portrayals of southern gentle-women, and Amanda and Laura Wingfield in The Glass Menagerie *are two striking examples, according to Falk in the following essay. Amanda is presented as an aging southern belle who romanticizes the past and fails to recognize the reality of her present situation, Falk contends. Laura is more sympathetically portrayed as a fragile misfit who needs protection and understanding, the author suggests.*

Like D.H. Lawrence, Tennessee Williams, the son of a Puritanical mother and a boisterous father, was strongly attached to his mother during a serious childhood illness, later rebelled against her moral restrictions, and glorified the sensual. Williams' studies of Southern gentlewomen, his most distinctive contribution to the American theater, develop this conflict between the Puritan and the Cavalier that he had first portrayed in his earlier poems, short stories, and plays. Amanda Wingfield and her daughter Laura of *The Glass Menagerie*, Blanche du Bois of *A Streetcar Named Desire*, Alma Winemiller of *Summer and Smoke* and of *Eccentricities of a Nightingale*, and Hannah Jelkes of *The Night of the Iguana* are sympathetic variations of the type. . . .

Signi Falk, "The Southern Gentlewoman," in *Tennessee Williams*, 2nd ed. Boston: Twayne Publishers, 1978, pp. 46–75. Copyright © 1978 Cengage Learning. All rights reserved. Reproduced by permission.

In the production notes to the first published edition of *The Glass Menagerie*, Williams expressed the hope that this memory play in seven sharply recreated scenes would anticipate "a new plastic theater" that would replace "the exhausted theater of realistic conventions." Since poetic imagination could transform the concrete into an inner truth, he rejected photographic realism in favor of unconventional techniques. In this same preface, his stage directions call for screen devices to project images and legends, for nostalgic music to enhance emotional overtones, and for shafts of light in different intensities to strengthen the dominant mood of a scene.

Sometimes the narrator who introduces the scene and sometimes the actor in it, Tom sets the play in the 1930s. He describes Americans as going their blind way, dancing, making love, and as being mildly disturbed by labor troubles at the same time that the Spaniards are being methodically slaughtered at Guernica. A lonely soul, Tom is ignored or slightly ridiculed by his fellow workers at the plant where he works until the big Irishman, Jim O'Connor, pays attention to him.

Amanda Fails to Accept Reality

Amanda Wingfield, the mother who is addicted to bromides and fantasies, is a middle-aged Southern belle. Garrulous and at times comic in her obsessions, her view of life is warped by her Puritan strictures; but she lives in delusions about her girlhood conquests. Her husband, present only in a blown-up photograph over the mantle, is described as a telephone man who fell in love with long distance and left his family for good. Deceived as a girl by his smile and uniform, she currently deludes herself about the seventeen gentleman callers who presented themselves one Sunday afternoon, men who later achieved wealth.

Just as willfully, Amanda ignores present reality. Overanxious to have her daughter, Laura, securely married, she refuses to recognize the girl's painful shyness or to admit to her slightly crippled leg. She insists that Laura not refer to herself as a cripple, that she speak only of a "little defect," and that she distract attraction from it by developing charm and vivacity. Amanda has known what can happen to a Southern girl without a home of her own: "I know so well what becomes of unmarried women who aren't prepared to occupy a position. I've seen such pitiful cases in the South—barely tolerated spinsters living upon the grudging patronage of sister's husband or brother's wife!—stuck away in some little mouse-trap of a room—encouraged by one in-law to visit another—little birdlike women without any nest—eating the crust of humility all their life!"

Tom Is a Dreamer

Though Amanda is proud of Tom, she is insensitive to his position. She carps at him continually about his eating habits, his smoking, his going to the movies, his late hours, his boredom with the warehouse job, and his need for adventure. When he tries to explain that man is by instinct a fighter, a hunter, and a lover, she is offended by his language. Reflecting her early twentieth-century Puritanism, Amanda believes that Christian adults should be concerned with things of the mind and spirit and leave dirty words like *instinct* for monkeys and pigs. Another argument erupts over a D.H. Lawrence novel that Tom brought home from the library, for she dismisses this writer as insane and offensive.

Exasperated by his mother's everlasting nagging about his running away to the movies, Tom bluntly tells her how much he detests the life he is leading. He is appalled by the idea of spending fifty-five years cooped up in a celotex workroom with fluorescent lights for sixty-five dollars a month; of waking up every morning to her maddening cheerfulness, "Rise and shine, rise and shine"; of returning each day to the warehouse, over and over again, in order to record shoe numbers. He would rather be dead. Tom Wingfield is a poet-dreamer who is something like his creator who also struggled against routine and conformity. Tom's shoe factory job, the poetry writing, the cramped living quarters, and the very close relationship with the sister are all echoes of Williams' own experience.

Laura Is Gentle and Reclusive

Laura, the morbidly shy and overly delicate sister, is as fragile as the little glass ornaments and phonograph records that are her escape. Through her timidity, her suffering from the friction between Tom and Amanda, and her retreat into a world of dreams, Laura evokes genuine sympathy; she is the one who must be cared for, loved, and understood. Her charm and delicacy win the audience, just as they have won her brother. Perceptive of others' feelings, Laura senses her mother's need to romanticize her past and so stands as a buffer between the mother and son. For one so sensitive and shy, the clanking brace on her leg is torture. During her final semester in high school, she becomes nervously ill, fails her final examinations, and does not graduate. When her desperate mother spends fifty dollars on a secretarial course, Laura becomes nauseated during the typing speed test. Amanda forces her to join a young people's church group where she might meet some nice boys. Because Laura won't or can't talk, the girl is humiliated.

The mother makes another attempt to provide for her daughter by asking Tom to find a clean-living, nondrinking suitor. When from his limited acquaintance he invites a warehouse friend to dinner, her hopes skyrocket. Tom admits that he has said nothing about Laura and tries to make his mother be a little more realistic:

TOM: Mother you mustn't expect too much from Laura.

AMANDA: What do you mean?

TOM: Laura seems all those things to you and me because she's ours and we love her. We don't even notice she's crippled any more.

Each of the characters in The Glass Menagerie *look at the titular figurines in this 1966 television production of the play.* © CBS Photo Archive/Getty Images.

AMANDA: Don't say crippled! You know that I never allow that word to be used!

TOM: But face the facts, Mother. She is and—that's not all—

AMANDA: What do you mean, not all?

TOM: Laura is very different from other girls.

AMANDA: I think the difference is all to her advantage.

TOM: Not quite all—in the eyes of others—strangers—she's terribly shy and lives in a world of her own and those things make her seem a little peculiar to people outside the house.

AMANDA: Don't say peculiar.

TOM: Face the facts. She is.

Refusing to listen, Amanda tries with grim feminine energy to change Laura into a pretty trap; for, on the ill-fated evening when the girl is so nervously ill that she cannot eat dinner, the determined mother crudely isolates the young man and her daughter.

Jim Has Energy but Lacks Imagination

Tom describes Jim O'Connor, the gentleman caller, as a high school hero; he was evidently one of those dynamic extroverts whose youth, looks, and enthusiasm won him the vote as the boy graduate most likely to succeed. Time and circumstances have proven otherwise, but he does work on self-improvement courses in public speaking and in radio engineering. Jim, the very average white-collar worker, the not too imaginative American, is, ironically, the boy whom Laura has secretly loved for years; but her only association with him has been his several pictures in the high school annual.

Amanda's planned evening, begun in panic for Laura, becomes her dream made real for a brief time. It is a beautiful love scene set to candlelight—of necessity, since the electricity was turned off because Tom had appropriated the money to buy a merchant seaman's membership. When Laura brings out the high school annual with all its romantic memories, she restores some of the old excitement to the disappointed hero. He brashly analyzes Laura as a victim of an inferiority complex, talks to her as if he were addressing his public-speaking class in evening school, and is completely impervious to the reactions of his little one-girl, wide-eyed audience. He says that she has magnified her trouble with the brace, that she ought to forget it, and that she should think of herself as superior in some way. Jim then talks in big terms about his own future plans, becomes a little abashed at his own egotism, and then remembers his evening class lesson about success that comes from interest in other people.

Laura responds to Jim's encouragement by showing him her precious glass collection. After she picks up her dearest treasure, the thirteen-year old unicorn, she points to the single horn on his forehead; she admits that he is extinct, but she asserts that she loves him because he must feel lonesome. This little glass figure is a living thing to her; she talks about his accepting without complaint his companions—horses without horns:

LAURA: Hold him over the light, he loves the light! You see how the light shows through him?

JIM: It sure does shine!

LAURA: I shouldn't be partial, but he is my favorite one.

JIM: What kind of thing is this one supposed to be?

LAURA: Haven't you noticed the single horn on his forehead?

JIM: A unicorn, huh?

LAURA: Mn—hmmmmmmmmm.

JIM: Unicorns, aren't they extinct in the modern world?

LAURA: I know!

JIM: Poor little fellow, he must feel sort of lonesome.

LAURA (*smiling*): Well, if he does he doesn't complain about it. He stays on the shelf with some horses that don't have horns and all of them seem to get along nicely together.

Laura is carried away with the conversation, but Jim's attention is soon distracted by the music from across the alley. He gallantly asks Laura to dance; they take a few steps in a clumsy waltz and hit the table. There is a shatter of glass. The unicorn is broken.

LAURA: Now it is just like all the other horses.

JIM: It's lost its—

LAURA: Horn! It doesn't matter. Maybe it's a blessing in disguise.

JIM: You'll never forgive me. I bet it was your favorite piece of glass.

LAURA: I don't have favorites much. It's no tragedy, Freckles. Glass breaks so easily. No matter how careful you are.

Jim is won by Laura's unique charm, but he is even more impressed with his own power. Like the clumsy stumble-bum who broke the unicorn, and seemingly unaware of what has happened to the girl, he talks about making her proud and not shy. He kisses her and then realizes his mistake; for, seeing her bright, dazed look, he dimly senses her love for him. After he pops a mint into his mouth, he bluntly explains that another girl has strings on him. Unaware that he is destroying all the self-confidence that he might have built up in the girl, he talks of the power of love that has made a man of him. The playwright says of his heroine that the holy candles have been snuffed out, that her face has *"a look of almost infinite desolation."* Laura gently places the broken unicorn that has lost its unique quality and any resemblance to her in the hand of the big Irishman and closes his fingers around her favorite ornament. He seems unaware that he has broken not only her unicorn but also her heart.

When Amanda discovers the awful conclusion to her planned evening, she brutally accuses Tom of allowing them to make fools of themselves and of recklessly spending their slim resources; she has completely forgotten that Tom had tried to reason with her. When he leaves abruptly to escape to the movies, Amanda, left alone, comforts her wounded Laura; and her reassurances are strong enough to bring a smile to the girl's face. The tragic dignity of this brief scene, when Amanda's speech cannot be heard, recalls her earlier observation about Southern gentlewomen without a home of their own.

Tom, fired for writing poetry on the boss's time, leaves his home, as did his father, to find escape. He cannot succeed, for he finds in every city there is a reminder of his sister: "Oh, Laura, Laura, I tried to leave you behind me, but I am more faithful than I intended to be! I reach for a cigarette, I cross the street, I run into the movies or a bar, I buy a drink. I speak to the nearest stranger—anything that can blow your candles out! (*Laura bends over the candles.*)—for now the world is lit by lightning! Blow out your candles, Laura—and so goodbye—(*She blows the candles out.*)"

The Glass Menagerie Examines Responsibility and Guilt in Family Relationships

Alice Griffin

Alice Griffin is a professor emerita and former director of graduate studies in English at Lehman College of the City University of New York. She is the author of Understanding Lillian Hellman, Understanding Arthur Miller, *and* Understanding Tennessee Williams.

In The Glass Menagerie *Williams explores the roles of guilt and responsibility in family relationships, according to Griffin in the following essay. Although Amanda glorifies the past, she does not retreat into it but rather attempts to find solutions to her present-day problems, Griffin explains; however, Amanda's plans for her children are unrealistic and doomed to failure.*

With a lyricism new to the American stage and a theatricalism that would define his future works, Williams in *The Glass Menagerie* dramatizes responsibility and guilt in the family relationship and examines the question at its core: "Am I my brother's / sister's keeper?"

Williams Created "Plastic Theater"

With humor, grace, and compassion Williams looks back at his own family and through his unique alchemy transforms a single incident—the visit of a dinner guest—into a universal revelation about parent-child conflict and brother-sister bonding. The visit, casual for the guest, assumes near tragic proportions for the mother and sister.

Alice Griffin, "*The Glass Menagerie*," in *Understanding Tennessee Williams*. Columbia: University of South Carolina Press, 1995, pp. 21–44. Copyright © 1995 by University of South Carolina Press. All rights reserved. Reproduced by permission.

To express his universal truths Williams created what he termed plastic theater, a distinctive new style of drama. He insisted that setting, properties, music, sound, and visual effects—all the elements of staging—must combine to reflect and enhance the action, theme, characters, and language. The result is an artistic entity that Williams describes as "lyric" and "dynamic."

From *The Glass Menagerie*, with its final stage picture that haunts not only Tom but audiences as well, through *The Night of the Iguana*, with its celebration of compassion in an Eden-like setting, Williams displays his new type of theater. As he states in his "Production Notes," he seeks to break the constraints of the "exhausted" realistic plays of his day and to employ "poetic imagination" to represent "truth, life, or reality" through "transformation."

Transforming reality through stage magic begins with the son Tom's opening words: "Yes, I have tricks in my pocket, I have things up my sleeve. But I am the opposite of a stage magician. He gives you illusion that has the appearance of truth. I give you truth in the pleasant disguise of illusion." Here Williams also gives the audience poetry in the pleasant disguise of ordinary speech. The poetic devices of these opening lines—balance and antithesis, alliteration, repetition and rhythm—were new to conversational stage dialogue and were to characterize Williams's work to come. Symbolism and word play abound, like the telephone idiom Tom uses to describe his long-absent father: "a telephone man who fell in love with long distances. . . . The last we heard of him was a picture postcard . . . containing a message of two words: 'Hello—Goodbye!'"

Tom (Williams's first name was Thomas) introduces the other characters in the play, his mother, Amanda, his sister, Laura, and a gentleman caller, "the most realistic character in the play, being an emissary from a world of reality that we were somehow set apart from."

Amanda Is Laughable and Admirable

Amanda Wingfield is the first in a line of memorable women Williams will create, and, like the others, she is a many-faceted, unique individual. But Amanda is also a universal type, a mother with the characteristic qualities of devotion to her offspring and determination to survive for their sakes. She is, however, an extremist who carries these traits to their limits, and beyond. She may, like all mothers, nag Tom to eat more and Laura to do her homework, but only Amanda can chirp so cheerfully each morning, "Rise and shine!" to her weary son or urge him, in scene 1, "chew—chew! Animals have secretions in their stomachs which enable them to digest food without mastication, but human beings are supposed to chew their food before they swallow it down."

Although the family now lives in reduced circumstances in St. Louis on Tom's salary of sixty-five dollars a month as a warehouse clerk, Amanda never stops reminding her children of her own more affluent past. Reminiscing is a recognizable parental characteristic, but it is an obsession with Amanda. In his introduction to "The Characters" Williams says she is "clinging frantically to another time and place."

Retreating from the harsh reality of the Depression to the illusion of herself in the legendary Old South of elegant beaux and belles makes the present somehow more bearable for Amanda. Laura understands this, as she begs Tom, impatient with his mother's oft-told tale, to "let her tell it. She loves to tell it," as Amanda in scene 1 launches into the first of her arias about the past: "One Sunday afternoon in Blue Mountain—your mother received—*seventeen!*—gentlemen callers! . . . My callers were gentlemen—all! Among my callers were some of the most prominent young planters of the Mississippi Delta—planters and sons of planters!" The myth of the Old South, in which Amanda devoutly believes, was one of gracious living, family tradition, chivalry, and coquetry which lent a stability of time and place to those who partook of it, as

Thomas E. Porter points out [in his article "The Passing of the Old South"]. Alienation from place led to the "preoccupation with time" which affects Amanda as she constantly harks back to earlier days.

Strangely anachronistic in a 1930s tenement, Amanda's airs and graces are those of a woman brought up only to look attractive, behave graciously, and choose a husband from among many suitors. Although in her recollections she is sought after by many eligible young men (ironically, she tells Tom that "character" is important in choosing a mate), these happy courting days ended sadly. Unfortunately, her upbringing did not prepare her to choose a mate for qualities other than "charm," nor did it train her to earn her own living when her charming spouse deserted her. To supplement Tom's meager salary she has demonstrated brassieres at a department store for the fifty dollars' tuition for Laura at business school and now sells magazine subscriptions by phone to decorate the apartment for the expected dinner guest.

Despite her lapses into her earlier, more glorious days, Amanda does not live in the past—a luxury she could not afford. She recognizes that their situation is near desperate, but she is unable to accept Tom and Laura as they are. Laura is crippled, though Amanda insists on never allowing "that word to be used!" Tom, who hates his warehouse job, wants only to be left alone to write, but Amanda refuses to recognize or accept his creative work or even the books he reads: "That hideous book by that insane Mr. Lawrence. . . . I cannot control the output of diseased minds. . . . BUT I WON'T ALLOW SUCH FILTH BROUGHT INTO MY HOUSE!". Tom's escape is to go to the movies; a pastime Amanda resents. As Williams introduces Amanda in "The Characters," he notes that "there is much to admire in Amanda, and as much to love and pity as there is to laugh at. Certainly she has endurance and a kind of heroism, and though her foolishness makes her unwittingly cruel at times, there is tenderness in her slight person."

A World of Illusion

Delma Presley [in *The Glass Menagerie: An American Memory*] sees Amanda, along with Laura and even Jim, as "characters caught up in illusions of their own making": "All of them . . . have built their lives on insubstantial premises of deception." And it is Amanda "who always seems to reap the bitter consequences of deception," by her husband, by Laura (in going to the zoo instead of business school), by Tom (in using the light bill money to join the merchant seamen), and even, unwittingly, by the gentleman caller. One must keep in mind; however, that Amanda, despite her urging "gay deceivers" (bosom enhancers) upon Laura in scene 6, deceives no one except perhaps herself, for she really believes in her role as a Southern belle.

The visual image and its implications were as important to Williams as his dialogue: "When I write, everything is visual, as brilliantly as if it were on a lit stage." [as Williams told interviewer Dotson Rader in a 1981 *Paris Review* interview]. In scene 6 Amanda becomes a touching visual image of the futility of attempting to recreate the past in the present. Although she is now twice the age of the belle she was, she dons for the invited gentleman caller a "girlish frock of yellowed voile with a blue silk sash," which she found in an old trunk, wears her hair in ringlets, and carries a bunch of jonquils to revive the "legend of her youth . . . nearly." With dinner guest Jim, as if he were her suitor, she behaves with "girlish Southern vivacity . . . social charm, . . . gay laughter and chatter." The vignette is as gently humorous as it is pathetic.

As he will do with his future heroines, Williams gives Amanda a distinctive idiom. Her two long speeches to Jim in scene 6 are characteristic: "I've heard so much about you from my boy. I finally said to him, Tom—good gracious!—why don't you bring this paragon to supper? I'd like to meet this nice young man at the warehouse!—instead of just hearing him sing your praises so much! I don't know why my son is so stand-offish—that's not Southern behavior!" (Southern behavior in Amanda's view evidently did not value facts as much as style.) After one word from Jim and four from Tom, she expands on her "gracious living . . . . gentlemen callers . . . sons of planters" and marriage to a man who "travels and I don't even know where!" She is breathlessly loquacious, as if endless talking could stave off an unexpected Caller, who might just be gentlemanly enough to wait until she has finished.

Because most of his heroines are Southern, Williams can heighten what he observes to be the "natural eloquence" of Southern women. In Amanda's speeches critic Stark Young [writing in the April 16, 1945, *New Republic*] hears "the echo of great literature." Fearing Laura will be a spinster, Amanda in scene 2 onomatopoetically describes such women as "little birdlike women without any nest—eating the crust of humility all their life." The rhythm and meter in Amanda's speeches are often that of iambic pentameter: "Laura, come here and make a wish on the moon! . . . / A little silver slipper of a moon".

Although annoying at the time, Amanda's excesses can be viewed in retrospect by Tom with gentle humor—her self-dramatizing in scene 2 with Laura over her leaving the business college, her coquettish manner with Jim, and her two phone conversations. Amanda is at her best (and worst) in the telephone calls to Daughters of the American Revolution (DAR) friends to promote magazine subscriptions that might bring in extra money "to feather the nest and plume the bird," as Tom says. But in scene 3, beneath her gushing descriptions of the serial fiction—"a book that critics already compare to *Gone with the Wind*"—one senses a note of desperation.

Laura Is Based on Sister Rose

Only desperation could prompt Amanda's belief that fragile, withdrawn Laura could marry to find security in life. Aware of

Tom's letter from the merchant marine, Amanda warns him in scene 4 that, until Laura is "married, a home of her own, independent . . . . you've got to look out for your sister . . . . because she's young and dependent."

Based on Williams's own sister Rose, whose disability was mental rather than physical, Laura is a delicately drawn, haunting figure. Her defect has caused Laura to withdraw into her own world, lovingly tending her glass collection and playing her father's old phonograph records. Just as Amanda's arias recall her past, so the old songs like "Dardanella" and "Whispering" conjure up the absent father. In his introduction to "The Characters" Williams says of Laura that her "separation increases till she is like a piece of her own glass collection, too exquisitely fragile to move from the shelf."

In its beauty and luminous fragility the glass menagerie symbolizes Laura. She describes it to Jim in scene 7: "Little articles . . . ornaments mostly! Most of them are little animals made out of glass, the tiniest little animals in the world. Mother calls them a glass menagerie!" They are her escape mechanism, as the movies are Tom's and the past is Amanda's.

Despite the signs of Laura's increasing separation from reality, Amanda persists, as if forcing her daughter into activities that are "normal" will make her so. Amanda regards as a betrayal, not a warning signal, Laura's flight from business school, where she was sent to learn skills to obtain a job that would support her. So that Amanda would believe she was in school, Laura has spent nine hours a day wandering in cold parks and visiting the zoo rather than attending the school, where the typing speed test made her hands shake so, her fingers couldn't hit the right keys. In scene 2, when Amanda challenges her about this "deception," Laura can only reply, "It was the lesser of two evils."

Amanda's next attempt is even more unrealistic than her first—to invite to dinner a young man who would, like Amanda's gentleman callers, propose marriage. When in scene

2 Amanda suggests marriage as an alternative to a business career, Laura protests "*(in a tone of frightened apology)*: I'm—crippled!" Amanda, undaunted, insists: "Why, you're not crippled, you just have a little defect—hardly noticeable, even! When people have some slight disadvantage like that, they cultivate other things to make up for it—develop charm—and vivacity—and—*charm!* That's all you have to do!"

As he informs his mother in scene 5 that a gentleman caller is indeed coming to dinner, Tom tries to warn her that she "mustn't expect too much of Laura," who might "seem a little peculiar to people outside the house": "She lives in a world of her own—a world of little glass ornaments, Mother." In the play Laura's lameness is seen as the cause of her withdrawal from the world, but it is also a symbol of a more serious, mental condition such as that suffered by Williams's sister Rose. . . .

Laura Retreats Further

With great artistry Williams dramatizes the progression of Laura's initial shyness and withdrawal to her fright when she learns that the visitor is the same Jim O'Connor she had idolized in high school, to her "Terror"—the "legend" seen on the screen as Amanda insists that Laura appear at the table. When she does so, "She is obviously quite faint, her lips trembling, her eyes wide and staring. She moves unsteadily toward the table".

Williams's dramatic skills are evident both in the characterization of Jim and in the delineation of the action between him and Laura. As the short, magical sequence begins to unfold in scene 7, it is implied that the "long delayed but always expected something we live for" might just be possible for Laura. Jim is now a "high school hero" only to Laura; after graduation "his speed had definitely slowed"; he is now a warehouse clerk along with Tom. Ironically, despite Jim's lack of advancement, he epitomizes the American Dream. He is studying science and public speaking, getting "in on the ground floor. . . . Full steam—*Knowledge*—Zzzzp! *Money*—Zzzzzp!—*Power!* That's the cycle democracy is built on!" He even compares himself to Superman. But at the same time he is a true "gentleman" caller, gentle and understanding. As Laura and Jim, alone in the candlelight, chew gum, talk, and finally dance, Jim draws Laura out of her shell to speak about her glass collection and even to trust him holding the unicorn.

He kisses her gently and then realizes his mistake. But Laura is transformed: "She looks up, smiling. . . . Her look grows brighter even." Then Jim explains about his fiancée Betty. Laura "struggles visibly with her storm. . . . There is a look of almost infinite desolation." Williams conveys the desolation that such a shock would wreak upon a fragile mind by giving Laura only three more words of dialogue in the final scene; she places the unicorn in his hand as "A—souvenir . . ." (Williams's ellipsis) and utters "Yes," when Amanda wishes the hastily departing Jim good luck. Laura's reversion to an even greater withdrawal is indicated by her posture, visibly shrinking from the hurtful reality toward which she will never again venture. She "crouches beside the Victrola to wind it," as Amanda comments: "Things have a way of turning out so badly. I don't believe that I would play the Victrola." Amanda and Tom have their final argument, and he leaves for good.

As he recalls his mother and sister in his final speech, continuing the mood of nostalgia established at the opening, and the "sorrow" of the musical refrain called "Laura's music," Tom's sense of loss is all the greater. It is not only his loss of "yesteryear" (the first "legend" to appear on the backlighted screen) but Laura's loss, to which he responded with desertion, followed by everlasting guilt.

Throughout the drama Tom plays a double role. He is the son in the action as well as the narrator who looks back on the events of the past from the perspective of the present. As narrator, he introduces, explains, interprets, and comments ironically on the action: "The idea of getting a gentleman caller for Laura . . . . became an obsession," he says at the beginning of scene 3. "Like some archetype of the universal unconscious, the image of the gentleman caller haunted our small apartment."

As "the play is memory," and memory is selective, Tom's recollections of his mother center on their conflicts. In the opening scene she is nagging him about his table manners, and in the course of the play their quarrels mount in intensity until he leaves the family. Amanda has no sympathy with his "creative labor," interrupting his writing, challenging his moviegoing in scene 3: "What right have you got to jeopardize your job?" To her charge that he is selfish Tom replies: "You think I'm in love with the Continental Shoemakers? . . . Look! I'd rather somebody picked up a crowbar and battered out my brains—than go back mornings! I *go!* Every time you come in yelling that Goddamn '*Rise and Shine!*' '*Rise and Shine!*' I say to myself, 'How *lucky dead* people are!' But I get up. . . . I give up all that I dream of doing and being *ever!*" Tom's frustration is justified, but so are Amanda's fears that he will desert them, as his father did.

Williams has an unerring instinct for memorable endings that are not only inevitable but also high drama. As Tom delivers his curtain speech, Amanda and Laura are seen through a scrim in a tableau image that refuses to leave his mind. His guilt at his desertion of them, as he travels through the world, pursues him like Orestes' Furies [in Greek mythology]. . . .

While the glass collection is the most recurrent image of Laura, other symbols are the unicorn, blue roses, and candles. All three, like Laura, have no place in this world, being (successively) extinct, nonexistent, and anachronistic. Tom's final line is: "For nowadays the world is lit by lightning! Blow out your candles, Laura—and so goodbye. . . ." (Williams's ellipsis) as, behind the scrim, Laura blows the candles out, ending the play.

The Backdrop of the 1930s

The family tragedy is set against the larger social context of the country in the 1930s, when "the huge middle class of America was matriculating in a school for the blind," as Tom reports in his opening speech. There was revolution in Spain and, for the first time, aerial destruction of whole towns, like Guernica, while here, "there was only shouting and confusion . . . disturbances of labor, sometimes pretty violent, in otherwise peaceful cities." In scene 5 the tune "All the World is Waiting for the Sunrise!" drifts in from the Paradise Dance Hall, where, Tom notes, couples dance under "a large glass sphere," with "delicate rainbow colors," while "all the world was waiting for bombardments!" (Williams always chooses popular tunes that are both apt and symbolic.) As the destruction of World War II looms, escape-seeking society might be regarded as a macrocosm of the Wingfield family, where the women seek refuge in old traditions and old tunes, and Tom deserts them to wander the world, only to learn there is no escape.

Tom Escapes His Family, but Not His Memories

Tom Scanlan

Tom Scanlan was an associate professor of writing studies in the Department of Rhetoric at the University of Minnesota. He is the author of Family, Drama, and American Dreams.

Like other major American playwrights such as Eugene O'Neill and Arthur Miller, Tennessee Williams explores the theme of the conflict between society and family, states Scanlan in the following essay. Like Miller, Williams portrays characters who escape a dysfunctional family and are then haunted by their memories, Scanlan explains. Williams artfully symbolizes the destruction of a family through the two levels of the play—it is both played out in front of the audience and simultaneously presented as the memory of the son who escaped, Scanlan states.

Arthur Miller struggled to come to terms with the same family dilemma which [Eugene] O'Neill explored so fully. The American family had failed to achieve its natural harmony, and Miller's reaction was to search the relations between family and society for an answer. Tennessee Williams, too, has reacted to the failed family dream, but in a way opposite to Miller. An inward tendency dominates his dramatic world. He asserts the painful isolation of life against which his characters violently struggle, testing the inner psychological limits of individual existence. O'Neill has rendered this impulse dramatically by trapping the individual within the family, leaving him nowhere else to go, and thrusting him into an

Tom Scanlan, "Family and Psyche in *The Glass Menagerie*," in *Family, Drama, and American Dreams.* Westport, CT: Greenwood Press, 1978, pp. 156–58, 166–77. Copyright © 1978 by Tom Scanlan. All rights reserved. Reproduced by permission of ABC-CLIO, LLC, Santa Barbara, CA.

iterating cycle of family conflict and destruction. Williams's characters are not trapped in the same way. As in Miller they leave (or are driven out of) the warring family, but the memory of family haunts them relentlessly. Escape from family does not result in a struggle to find a new order to replace family, as in Miller; it means, instead, a desperate search for some anodyne to the pain of being bereft of family.

William's Characters Are Isolated

Rather than Miller's community togetherness or O'Neill's innocent home, William's characters will settle for a moment's peace and tenderness. When even that bare victory is not possible, sex and drugs are the (unsatisfactory) substitute. Those who are defeated possess the special sensitivity needed for that contact which allows a brief moment of surcease from the torment of life. But such sensitivity makes them all the more vulnerable. The most intense expression of their need for love and an end to loneliness is the memory of family, and increasingly William's characters settle for transient groupings which are no longer really families at all.

If in Williams the ideal of family harmony is reduced to brief gestures of kindness, the family itself is an arena wherein the life forces of sex and fecundity are at war with man's spirit. This would suggest that Williams is dissatisfied with the very conditions of existence (which he symbolizes in family life and family ideal). We can go so far as to say that for Williams the family is the primary expression of organized animal vitality antithetical to the life of the spirit. But we cannot go much beyond this generalization, for Williams does little to define the nature and content of this view. He accepts it rather unselfconsciously with no clear sense of the assumptions it entails. He concentrates, instead, on making the individual's painful relationship to his family vivid and theatrically evocative.

Williams Portrays the Interior World

William's concern with the interior psychological state repeatedly takes him past the boundaries of the realistic theater which O'Neill accepted in presenting the Tyrone family [in *Long Day's Journey into Night*] and which Miller tentatively exploited in the Loman family [in *Death of a Salesman*]. His is a drama which, in its emphasis on inner reality, moves further and more consistently than Miller or O'Neill toward the subjective. We have nearly left the domestic drama in talking about Tennessee Williams—nearly, but not quite. For if he moves from realism and from the family, he never quite abandons either. Indeed, part of the peculiarity of effect which Williams achieves depends on the maintenance of those connections. And in tracing their outlines, we are measuring the degree to which the realistic family situation continues to attract our playwrights, even those who are avowedly anti-realistic.

Williams's dramatic vision, as Esther Merle Jackson has usefully pointed out [in *The Broken World of Tennessee Williams*], can be seen to take its cue from the consciousness of one character in each play. Looked at in this way, Williams is projecting a lyric moment of that character which is, for him, the play itself. The technical device Williams uses to justify such an effect—and it is significant here that Williams wants a realistic justification—would be the point of view of a character whose perceptions are not limited in, say, the [Henry] Jamesian sense, but are distorted through memory, insanity, drugs, alcohol, or dreams. But even while we move into the bizarre or exaggerated situation emblematic of the gauzy mind of the protagonist, we are constantly aware that it approximates a realistic situation.

While Williams's family dramas are consistently more lyrical, looser, and more freewheeling than Miller's, they are not given over to the exploration of psychic irrationality. Nor do they exist primarily on the plane of symbolic abstraction or of idealization. Indeed, the whole matter of distortion—as important as it is to a precise understanding of Williams's tone—can be greatly overemphasized. Williams's plays, especially those dealing directly with the family, have a concreteness about them which suggests a calculated intensification of realistic conventions rather than a revolutionary break with these customs. Conversational prose speech, coherent and rationalized plot, everyday situations, and understandable motivation are not absent, but rather are slightly stylized to indicate the intense feelings they inadequately represent. Such exaggeration helps to emphasize the cruelty and destruction of family life. The reality of everyday family experience stands behind Williams's plays, and the effect of many of them depends on an audience saturated in realistic domestic drama. . . .

Williams Portrays Family Conflict

The major dilemmas of family life are imbedded in the dramatic action of Williams's plays, and the ideal that haunts his characters is family-related. Moreover, those plays which have been most successful artistically have been those mostly about the family—the plays up through *Cat on a Hot Tin Roof*; *Camino Real* is the only exception.

In the earlier plays Williams dramatized the family world in a state of collapse; in later ones family collapse is antecedent to the action. These two situations are combined in *The Glass Menagerie*, Williams's first successful play (and probably his most popular one). The play is a perfect fusion of the two subjects and so is a figure for Williams's entire career. In it the family is long lost and, also, we witness its struggle before it is lost. Williams captures the poignancy of family memories in a way all his own, without sacrificing the core of dramatic conflict which makes such memories less static.

The play is a prime example of Williams's artistry in establishing the relation between his own dramatic world and the conventions of realistic domestic drama to which his audience owes great allegiance, as he well knew. The play occurs in the mind of Tom Wingfield, who drifts in and out of the action both as narrator and participant in a peculiarly appropriate way. From the moment at the beginning when the scrim of the tenement wall dissolves and we enter the Wingfield's apartment, we are reminded of the household of so many family plays. The realistic convention of the fourth wall is evoked as Tom remembers his family.

Haunted by the Loss of His Family

Tom's evocation is self-conscious, for as "stage manager" he has control over the setting. But Tom is also at the mercy of his memories and irresistibly must relive them. The play keeps us poised between these two styles, these two times, throughout. This is, in fact, its strongest and most subtle conflict. Like Tom, we are continually tempted into the world of a realistic family struggle, but never allowed to enter it completely. The projections and lighting keep the effect slightly stylized during the scenes, the fragmented structure blocks us from too long an absorption in the action, and the reappearance of Tom as narrator forces us back to the present. It is Tom's final reappearance in this role, when the action of the memory play is completed, which releases the tension created between the two styles and dramatizes, in a final rush of emotion, the irretrievable loss of the family which Tom can never escape.

Tom cannot shake the memory of his family from his mind; the dissolution of time and space in the play—that is, in his consciousness—heightens the importance of what he is remembering to make it the most significant thing about his existence. What he remembers—the bulk of the play—centers around two lines of action. The first is his desire to escape from his family just as his father had done before him: "He was a telephone man who fell in love with long distances." Tom, a would-be writer, is caught between a domineering mother and a stultifying warehouse job. He escapes to the

In this still from the 1950 film adaptation of The Glass Menagerie, *Jim, the gentleman caller (played by Kirk Douglas), holds the broken unicorn given to him by the sensitive Laura (played by Jane Wyman).* © United Archives GmbH/Alamy.

porch, to the movies, to the saloon. And finally, in the end, we learn that he has followed his father out into long distances. The second line of action, the principal one, concerns his mother, Amanda, and her attempts to establish some kind of life for Tom's crippled sister, Laura. Amanda pins her hopes on getting "sister" married, after Laura fails because of painful shyness to continue in business school. A "gentleman caller" is found, Jim O'Conner, "an emissary from the world of reality," but all of Amanda's hopes are crushed as he turns out to be already engaged.

The plot is slight stuff, as Williams himself knew. The effect of the play derives in part from the contrast between its two lines of action. Amanda is given over to memories of her past life of happiness as a young southern debutante in Blue Mountain, Mississippi, where on one incredible Sunday she had seventeen gentlemen callers. She imitates the manners and graciousness of those days, a faintly ludicrous parody of southern gentility, the played-out tradition of the antebellum South and its family of security. But she has spirit, too, and responds to the problems of raising two children in a St. Louis tenement during the Depression. Her practicality is what gives her dignity; as she cares for Laura we realize how much Amanda herself needs to be cared for. Her refusal to give in to her nostalgia, even while she indulges in it, enhances her character and makes us susceptible to her longing.

Tom is smothered by such a woman. He fights with her, in part, because she continually tells him what to do: how to eat; how to sleep; how to get ahead. But he fights, also, because her standards represent the conventionality of family responsibility:

AMANDA: Where are you going?

TOM: I'm going to the *movies!*

AMANDA: I don't believe that lie!

[Tom crouches toward her, overtowering her tiny figure. She backs away, gasping.]

TOM: I'm going to opium dens! Yes, opium dens, dens of vice and criminals, hang-outs, Mother. I've joined the Hogan Gang, I'm a hired assassin, I carry a tommy-gun in a violin case! I run a string of cat-houses in the Valley! They call me

Killer, Killer Wingfield, I'm leading a double-life, a simple, honest warehouse worker by day, by night a dynamic *czar* of the *underworld, Mother.* I go to gambling casinos, I spin away fortunes on the roulette table! I wear a patch over one eye and a false mustache, sometimes I put on green whiskers. On those occasions they call me—*El Diablo!* Oh, I could tell you things to make you sleepless! My enemies plan to dynamite this place. They're going to blow us all sky-high some night! I'll be glad, very happy, and so will you! You'll go up, on a broomstick, over Blue Mountain with seventeen gentlemen callers! You ugly—babbling old—*witch.* . . .

He can no more accept her memories of genteel home life in Blue Mountain than he can the spirit with which she has managed to carry on. Both suffocate him. The dead family world of the past is as stultifying as the present. Tom feels the need to escape both:

You know it don't take much intelligence to get yourself into a nailed-up coffin, Laura. But who in hell ever got himself out of one without removing one nail?

[As if in answer, the father's grinning photograph lights up. The scene dims out.]

The absent father, who still represents the memory of romantic family love to Amanda, is the possibility of romantic escape from family to Tom. He loves his sister Laura, yet he will not accept the responsibility for her which Amanda demands of him. The Wingfields are only a ghost of the family of security, but even this demand to be close-knit repels the restless Tom.

Sympathetic to Society's Misfits

Tom's love for Laura needs to be emphasized, I think, not only because it is one part of the final image of the play—the moment of revelation toward which the action tends—but because it shows Williams's interest in the special qualities of those whom the world has hurt. They are the delicate and fragile people, too sensitive to be able to withstand the crude and harsh necessities by which life drives us along. They have an extraordinary awareness of hidden, almost mystical, qualities of spiritual beauty; and this openness dooms them to be crushed or perverted by the animal vigor of the world.

Laura's specialness is seen largely in contrast with Jim, her gentleman caller. He is, by all odds, the kindest of Williams's emissaries from reality, perhaps because his faith in the American dream of self-improvement and success is so complete as to be itself a touching illusion:

JIM [*Going after him*]: You know, Shakespeare—I'm going to sell you a bill of goods!

TOM: What goods?

JIM: A course I'm taking.

TOM: Huh?

JIM: In public speaking! You and me, we're not the warehouse type.

TOM: Thanks—that's good news. But what has public speaking got to do with it?

JIM: It fits you for—executive positions!

TOM: Awww.

JIM: I tell you it's done a helluva lot for me.

[*Image on screen: Executive at his desk.*]

Williams mocks Jim just enough in the use of the slide projection so that we need not take him seriously, yet he makes Jim's naïveté spring from high spirits and an openheartedness which is endearing. He is healthy, happy, and full of hope, but set next to Laura and her needs he is crude, clumsy, and shallow:

> You know what I judge to be the trouble with you? Inferiority complex! Know what that is? That's what they call it when someone low-rates himself!

So much for the intricacies of the human personality. To Jim, Laura's problems are easily solved and he sets about, in his well-intentioned way, to cure her. First, he persuades her to dance; and then, caught up himself in the romance of the moment, he kisses her. But Laura needs more than a kiss, more in fact than Jim could ever give her. She needs a tenderness and love that she will never find. Her needs are so great that to satisfy them would mean altering the real world to fit her, changing it into a world like that inhabited by her glass animals, full of delicacy, beauty, and tender harmony.

When this incompatible couple waltzes into the glass menagerie, they begin to destroy it. At first, Laura does not mind. She is too thrilled with the prospect of being normal to care whether her glass unicorn has lost its distinctive horn. But the accident warns us of what Jim awkwardly confesses after the kiss—that he has made a mistake and will see her no more:

> I wish that you would—say something.
>
> [*She bites her lip which was trembling and then bravely smiles. She opens her hand again on the broken glass ornament. Then she gently takes his hand and raises it level with her own. She carefully places the unicorn in the palm of his hand, then pushes his fingers closed upon it.*]
>
> What are you—doing that for? You want me to have him?— Laura?
>
> [*She nods.*]
>
> What for?
>
> LAURA: A—souvenir. . . .

Laura now knows that she belongs to a different world from Jim. He wandered into a zoo of exotic animals, but that was on his day off and he must return to the workaday world.

There will be no normal love of marriage and family for Laura nor for any of the Wingfields. Laura is too tender, too special, too fragile like her glass menagerie. It is Tom's painful sensitivity to Laura's predicament which makes him love her and which drives him from her. But he cannot escape Laura. The necessity of leaving her and the guilt over doing so, haunt him:

Oh, Laura, Laura, I tried to leave you behind me, but I am more faithful than I intended to be! I reach for a cigarette, I cross the street, I run into the movies or a bar, I buy a drink, I speak to the nearest stranger—anything that can blow your candles out!

[*Laura bends over the candles.*]

For nowadays the world is lit by lightning! Blow out your candles, Laura—and so good-bye. . . .

[*She blows the candles out.*]

Laura's painful encounter with the world's lightning represents all of the Wingfields. Amanda's last glance at her husband's picture reveals as much of her as does Tom's final speech of him. The family is the supreme case of love trying to struggle against the world, and the family fails. Fundamentally romantic, Williams evokes the beauty of failure, the beauty which must fail. . . .

In *The Glass Menagerie* Williams consciously manipulated his subject matter and his tone, playing off the oppressiveness of the family of security against a teasing stylized realism. He did not grapple with the assumptions beneath the conflicting claims of personal freedom and security, nor did he construct a dramatic action which defined them. Rather, he relied on the evocative power of family strife, running the risk of being merely agitated and pathos-filled as in the soap opera. His family victims are at their most vivid at those points where they are both caught up in their lyrical self-indulgence and at the same time aware of the difficulty in communicating to those around them what they truly feel.

Williams does not test the family attitudes which are his subject. He has evoked family fears and frustrations without probing them. But it is important to recognize the genuine, if limited, appeal of Williams's strategy. He has asked us to see his plays as artifice and as reports on reality. And he has used the artificial, "plastic" elements both to intensify and to relieve the intensity of the family struggles. This paradox is a most intriguing one. He has counted on our familiarity with the family drama, reminded us of it, and then eluded its more rigid restrictions. He has been a realist, if only in part, to refresh our response to the dilemmas of family life. His best plays remind us of our quest for relatedness and independence and so depend on, and contribute to, the very tradition of American domestic drama which he proposed to escape.

The Glass Menagerie
Is a Personal, Social,
and Religious Tragedy

Roger B. Stein

Roger B. Stein is a retired professor of the history of art at the University of Virginia. He has held Guggenheim and Fulbright fellowships and is the author of John Ruskin and Aesthetic Thought in America, 1840–1900.

The members of the Wingfield family are isolated from each other and from society as a whole, maintains Stein in the following selection. The play is set in the 1930s—a time when America was still mired in the Great Depression and about to become embroiled in World War II. Just as the Wingfield family is in shambles, so is the American dream, Stein contends. There is also religious symbolism in The Glass Menagerie, *the author explains. According to Stein, the characters are abandoned by God, with no hope of redemption.*

The Glass Menagerie (1945) was Tennessee Williams' first major theatrical success. Over the years he has written much, some of high quality indeed, but nothing better than this play which established him as an important post-war playwright. "The dramatist of frustration," John Gassner dubbed him in 1948 after *Streetcar* [*A Streetcar Named Desire*], but unlike most of his later plays, *The Glass Menagerie* projects not a series of violent confrontations leading to catastrophe but a vision of lonely human beings who fail to make contact, who are isolated from each other and from society, and who seem ultimately abandoned in the universe.

Roger B. Stein, "*The Glass Menagerie* Revisited: Catastrophe Without Violence," *Western Humanities Review*, vol. 18, Spring 1964, pp. 141–53. Copyright © 1964, The Estate of Roger B. Stein. All rights reserved. Reproduced by permission.

What holds the play together are Tom's remembrances of things past, not plot or characterization. Tom, the poet-narrator and author's surrogate, called "Shakespeare" in the warehouse, organizes the drama symbolically through language and image. This is the "new plastic theatre" of which Williams spoke in his production notes, a revelation not through dramatic struggle but through the allusive power of the word, the accretion of symbolic clusters which bear the meaning, reinforced dramaturgically through lighting, music, the distancing devices of a narrator and, as originally planned, of screen images.

Fragility in a Cruel World

The glass menagerie is itself the most obvious organizing symbol. It embodies the fragility of Laura's world, her search for beauty, it registers sensitively changes in lighting and stands in vivid contrast to the harshness of the outer world which can (and does) shatter it so easily. The unicorn can become the gift to Jim the Gentleman Caller, whose anticipation and appearance form the plot of the play, only when it has lost its mythical uniqueness, the horn, when dream becomes momentarily possibility before it is obliterated at the end. The magic of Prince Charming's kiss can not work ("Stumblejohn," he brands himself in the published version of the play, taking on for the moment Laura's crippled condition). The "little silver slipper of a moon" on which Amanda has asked Laura to wish becomes an ironic image of Laura's isolated condition, but Amanda, wrapped up in her own illusions and selling magazine subscriptions and brassieres (like the "Gay Deceivers" with which she tries to stuff Laura before Jim appears) prefers to believe not in Tom's favorite D.H. Lawrence, but in Cinderella and courtly love and *Gone With the Wind*, the novel to which she compares Bessie May Harper's latest effort in *The Homemaker's Companion*. The ironies of the allusive imagery proliferate: Amanda's heroic efforts as homemaker are unsuc-

The Wingfield family eats together in this scene from a 1945–46 production of The Glass Menagerie. © Bettmann/Corbis.

cessful (the father appears only as a happy doughboy photographic image), and Margaret Mitchell's depression romance about the desirable Scarlett O'Hara in a lost Eden, a South fantasized in the national imagination during the Depression, only makes Laura look more forlorn. Finally one may note that the title image itself of *Gone With the Wind* underlines the evanescent quality of this dream and all of the Wingfields' illusions. As such, it points directly to the last line of the play and Tom's injunction to "Blow out your candles, Laura."

On the level of plot, this widening circle of reference enhances the credibility of the dramatic situation. Given Amanda's sham version of idealized love and a fantasy past, how could the Gentleman Caller's visit be other than a failure? Despite Amanda's dress which is "historical almost," despite the attempt to live in the nineteenth century when the electric power goes off, Jim is not Rhett Butler but an "emissary from a world of reality," as Tom calls him, an engaged twentieth-century man on vacation. The flickering candlelight of Jim's scene with Laura is not enough to sustain the illusion; at the end of their scene this illusion collapses and we are left in darkness.

The Shattered American Dream

But *The Glass Menagerie* is built upon more than the poignant plot of illusion and frustration in the lives of little people. Williams has deepened the losses of individuals by pointing to social and even spiritual catastrophe. The time of the play is 1939, as the narrative frame makes explicit both at the beginning and the end. The life of illusion is not confined to the Wingfields alone. As Tom says, "the huge middle class of America was matriculating in a school for the blind." What he calls the "social background" of the play has an important role. The international backdrop is Guernica and the song America sings is "The World is Waiting for the Sunrise," for the sober truth is that America is still in the depression and on the brink of war. The note of social disaster runs throughout the drama, fixing the lives of individuals against the larger canvas.

Amanda's anxieties are in large part economic and there is money behind many of her illusions: her mythical suitors were all wealthy men, as are her magazine heroes; she computes the money Tom would save by giving up smoking. When Tom complains of the grimness of life in the shoe factory, she replies, "Try and you will SUCCEED!" If this is another of Amanda's illusions, it is one shared by her fellow Americans, for "try and you will succeed" is the traditional motto of the American dream of success, the theme of confident self-reliance canonized in the romances of Horatio Alger.

It is not Amanda, however, but Jim, the emissary from reality, who is the chief spokesman for the American dream. To Jim the warehouse is not a prison but a rung on the ladder toward success. He believes in self-improvement through education, and the lecture on self-confidence which he reads to Laura is part of the equipment of the future executive. He is awed by the fortune made in chewing gum and rhapsodizes on the theme of the future material progress of America: "All that remains is for the industry to get itself under way! Full steam—*Knowledge—Zzzzzp! Money—Zzzzzp! Power!* That's the cycle democracy is built on!"

Yet when the theme of success is superimposed upon the lives of the characters, the social irony emerges. Father was not the successful businessman, but a telephone man who "fell in love with long distances." Tom, the substitute father, refuses to pay the light bill, plunges his family into darkness, and then runs out, and Amanda sells subscriptions and brassieres only at the loss of her dignity. Jim's own dream of success seems to have reached its peak in high school. (Williams later explored this theme more fully in *Cat on a Hot Tin Roof.*) The trek upward through the depression years is disappointing, but the indomitable optimist is not discouraged.

The experience of the 1930s did not turn Williams into a proletarian writer or social realist, but it did open up for him a darker vision of American life which he suggests to his audience but which is denied to his characters, still "matriculating in a school for the blind": a belief that the American dream is itself a sham and a failure. In his essay "The Catastrophe of Success," Williams said that "the Cinderella story is our favorite national myth, the cornerstone of the film industry if not of the Democracy itself." The social catastrophe inherent in *The Glass Menagerie* lies precisely in the fact that Laura is *not* Cinderella: the silver slipper does not finally fit, and Jim is not Prince Charming but one of the innumerable Americans who would soon be moving overseas in troop ships. As Tom says at the end, "for nowadays the world is lit by lightning! Blow out your candles, Laura—and so goodbye. . . ." The world which had been waiting for the sunrise burst with bombardments instead, and the lives of the Wingfields at the end are absorbed in the larger social tragedy.

A World with No Hope of Redemption

Williams goes even further than this, however. The end of the play involves more than just the snuffing out of Laura's hope; it is even more than social tragedy. It is a *Gotterdammerung* [an apocalypse]. For the candles and the lightning which close the play have appeared together before. We are told by Amanda that the candelabrum "used to be on the altar at the church of the Heavenly Rest: It was melted a little out of shape when the church burnt down. Lightning struck it one spring." Amanda's comment opens up another dimension of the drama, and reminds us that Williams, inheritor of a Southern religious tradition which includes writers like [William] Faulkner and Robert Penn Warren, has persistently drawn upon the language of Christian symbolism to define his characters' human situations. Amanda's quiet comment is a far cry from the hysterical ravings of the defrocked Reverend T. Lawrence Shannon in *Night of the Iguana* about wanting "to go back to the church and preach the gospel of God as Lightning and Thunder." The pervasive religious overtones of *The Glass Menagerie* never obscure the literal line of the story or seem self-conscious, as they frequently do in the later plays. Ultimately they try to locate the catastrophe at the end beyond human pathos and social tragedy.

Williams' stage directions clearly indicate his intention. The lighting for Laura should resemble that "used in early religious portraits of female saints or madonnas." The scene where Tom tells his mother that a Gentleman Caller will appear Williams entitles "Annunciation." The dressing of Laura for the Caller's appearance should be "devout and ritualistic." During her scene with Jim she is lit "inwardly with altar candles," and when Jim withdraws after kissing her Williams informs us that the "holy candles in the altar of Laura's face have been snuffed out. There is a look of almost infinite desolation."

Those overtones extend beyond Williams' hints to the director and become part of the fabric of dramatic action. The first scene in both the acting version and the library edition of the play opens on this note. In the former, Amanda narrates her "funny experience" of being denied a seat in the Episcopal church because she has not rented a pew. The idea of the Wingfields' exclusion from Christian ceremony is established thus at the outset, and it is underlined by the ensuing talk of digesting food, mastication, and salivary glands. In the Wingfield apartment, eating is an animal process only; it lacks ritual significance. The library edition opens with Amanda's call to Tom, "We can't say grace until you come to the table," and then moves on to the question of digestion. The lines are different, but their import is the same. When the Gentleman Caller comes, the scene is repeated, only this time it is Laura whose absence holds up "grace."

Amanda, who condemns instinct, and urges Tom to think in terms of the mind and spirit, as "Christian adults" do, is often characterized in Christian terms. Her music, in the library edition, is "Ave Maria." As a girl she could only cook angel food cake. She urges Laura, "Possess your soul in patience," and then speaks of her dress for the dinner scene as "resurrected" from a trunk. Her constant refrain to Tom is "Rise an' Shine," and she sells subscriptions to her friends by waking them early in the morning and then sympathizing with them as "Christian martyrs." Laura is afraid to tell her mother she has left the business school because "when you're disappointed, you get that awful suffering look on your face, like the picture of Jesus' mother in the museum!"

The next picture Laura mentions is the one of Jim in the yearbook. Though the context seems secular enough at this point—Jim is a high school hero—his religious function emerges later on. In the "Annunciation" scene, when Amanda learns that the Gentleman Caller's name is O'Connor, she says, "that, of course, means fish—tomorrow is Friday!" The remark functions not only literally, since Jim is Irish Catholic, but also figuratively, for the fish is the traditional symbol of Christ. In a very real sense both Amanda and Laura are searching for a Savior who will come to help them, to save them, to give their drab lives meaning.

Tom is unable to play this role himself. Though he appears as the angel of the Annunciation, he denies the world of belief and in a bitter speech to his mother calls himself "El Diablo." With him Christian terms appear only as imprecations: "what in Christ's name" or "that God damn Rise and Shine." When Tom returns home drunk one night, he tells Laura of a stage show he has seen which is shot through with Christian symbolism, none of which he perceives. Here the magician, Malvolio, whose name suggests bad will, dislike, or even hate, plays the role of the modern Christ. He performs the miracle of turning water into wine and then goes on to blasphemy by turning the wine into beer and then whiskey. He also produces his proper symbol, the fish, but it is gold-fish, as if stained by modern materialism. Most important, he escapes from a nailed coffin. But Tom reads the symbolism of this trick in personal terms only. When Laura tries to keep him from awakening Amanda, Tom retorts:

> Goody, goody! Pay 'er back for all those "Rise an' Shines."
> You know it don't take much intelligence to get yourself into
> a nailed-up coffin, Laura. But who in hell ever got himself
> out of one with-out removing one nail?

The illumination of the father's photograph at this point suggests one answer to this question, but the pattern of Christian imagery in the drama, especially when reinforced here by the "Rise an' Shine" refrain, should suggest to us another answer—the resurrection itself—which Tom's rejection of Christian belief prevents him from seeing.

Williams's Vision Is Bleak

It remains therefore for Jim to come as the Savior to this Friday night supper. The air of expectancy is great, with the ritualistic dressing of Laura, the tension, and the oppressive heat. Jim's arrival is marked by the coming of rain, but the hopes of fertility and renewal which this might suggest are soon dashed. Laura's attempt to come to the dinner table is a failure, signaled by a clap of thunder, and Tom's muttered grace, "For these and all thy mercies, God's Holy Name be praised," is bitterly ironic, mocked by what follows. The only paradise within reach is Paradise Dance Hall, with its "Waste Land" mood of slow and sensuous rhythms and couples kissing behind ashpits and telephone poles, "the compensation for lives that passed . . . without any change or adventure," as Tom remarks. The failure of electric power after dinner—previsioning the blackout of the world—leads to Amanda's joking question, "Where was Moses when the lights went off?" This suggests another savior who would lead his people from the desert into the promised land, but the answer to her question is "In the dark."

Jim's attempt to play the modern savior is an abysmal failure. In the after-dinner scene, he offers Laura the sacrament—wine and "life-savers," in this case—and a Dale Carnegie version of the Sermon on the Mount—self-help rather than divine help—but to no avail. At the end of the play Laura and Amanda are, as the joke bitterly reminds us, "in the dark," and Tom's last lines announce the final failure, the infinite desolation: "For nowadays the world is lit by lightning. Blow out your candles, Laura—and so goodbye. . . ."

Here as elsewhere in his plays Williams draws upon his frightened characters' preference for soft candlelight to harsh daylight or electric bulbs, not only because it serves him dramaturgically to establish his conception of a new plastic theater where evanescent characters and images flicker across the stage momentarily, but also because his characters so often want to withdraw from the blinding light of reality into the softer world of illusion. At the end of *The Glass Menagerie*, however, the blackout is even more catastrophic, for it only envelops the Laura of Tom's memory and serves as another reminder of the blackout of war which shrouds the world: it is also the denial of any final "Rise an' Shine" for these frail creatures. The church has been struck by lightning, and all hope of resurrection has been lost in this damned universe where belief turns into metaphor, where humankind seems abandoned by its God, and where the echoes of prayer are heard only in blasphemy or irony. The bleakness of Williams' vision in *The Glass Menagerie* is complete. If Tom is released finally, it is in the words of Job, "And I only am escaped alone to tell thee." It is as the author's surrogate, as writer and chronicler of catastrophe, that he emerges at the end.

Postscript 1976

Published criticism of *The Glass Menagerie* since this essay was originally written in 1964 has confirmed in other particulars my sense of the importance of the religious language of the drama, and my interpretation, in turn, has been used to attack Marxist readings of the play as a dramatization of the disintegration of a lower middle class family under a ruthless capitalist system during the Depression. It is a tribute to the play's richness that it has stimulated both kinds of criticism. What I would emphasize now in rethinking these issues is that a Marxist analysis of the play, though incomplete, is both ideologically accurate and descriptively useful. Williams did serve his aesthetic apprenticeship during the 1930s, and in the first part of his opening description of the apartment building he does point us towards a class analysis of "this largest and fundamentally enslaved section of American society." But this intention loses force in the last few words of the paragraph.

Williams' understanding of and compassion for the illusions of the Wingfields are based upon an implicit recognition that work in America is alienating drudgery: Rubicam's Business College for Laura, selling illusions for Amanda, Continental Shoes for Tom ("the warehouse is where I work, not where I know people," he tells Amanda, with, as it turns out, devastating consequences for Laura). They are indeed victims of a larger social failure, for humane democratic values have been redefined and inverted by Jim, the economic system's apologist, as a use of knowledge to gain power and money. In this Depression world, as Tom tells us, it takes a war to make adventure available to the masses, to release them from the social trap. Which is of course precisely what happened.

In the light of these social clarifications, it seems to me now that Williams' religious language in the play becomes—however unconsciously—a strategic mode for evading the implications of his social analysis, about which, like Amanda ("We live in such a mysterious universe, don't we?"), he is finally muddled. If his sense of cosmic catastrophe and of the metaphysical abandonment of his characters in the universe is, as I have shown, in some ways a great dramatic and linguistic strength of the play, it is from another point of view a typical weakness of Williams and American writers in general. Failing in their art to explore humankind adequately in society, they shift responsibility for the human condition to the divine and write metaphysical romances rather than trenchant social drama, in a series of dramatic gestures which fluctuate between Byronic [characteristic of the works of Romantic poet Lord Byron] defiance and ultimate despair. This weakness is especially apparent in Williams' later plays, which frequently exploit what I would call the romance of violence. The greatness of *The Glass Menagerie*, as art and as human statement, still lies in Williams' ability at that point in his career to sustain a sense of the individual, the social, and the religious dimensions of our experience poised in delicate poetic balance.

A Broken Family Symbolizes the Broken American Dream

C.W.E. Bigsby

C.W.E. Bigsby is a professor of American studies at the University of East Anglia and is the award-winning author of several novels and books on British and American culture.

The Glass Menagerie *captures a moment of cataclysmic change for the Wingfield family that reflects the social change that was occurring in the world, explains Bigsby in the following article. He maintains that Amanda's efforts to secure a better life for her children are in vain—the potential suitor for her daughter Laura turns out to be engaged and her son Tom deserts the family as his father had before him. The Wingfields' personal drama is played out against the backdrop of the Great Depression, a time, as Bigsby describes, when the optimism of the Roaring Twenties had given way to the grim reality of economic disaster for many in America and the specter of war looming in Europe.*

[The Wingfield's apartment] is both literally and metaphorically a trap which Tom and his mother, at least, wish to escape, but the determinism is not primarily presented as politically or socially rooted. The alienation and despair go deeper than this. [Williams's] characters are, beyond anything, the victims of fate (Laura), of time (Amanda), and of a prosaic and destructive reality. However, the social and political backdrop is not as irrelevant as it may appear.

C.W.E. Bigsby, "Entering *The Glass Menagerie*," in *The Cambridge Companion to Tennessee Williams*, ed. Matthew C. Roudané. New York: Cambridge University Press, 1997, pp. 29–44 (edited version). Copyright © 1997 Cambridge University Press. All rights reserved. Reproduced by permission.

The Present Day Is Bleak

The Wingfields live on credit. The electricity is cut off following Tom's failure to pay the bill. Amanda scrapes together money by demonstrating brassieres at a local store, itself a humiliation for a woman of her sensibility. Otherwise she has to suffer the embarrassment of selling subscriptions to women's magazines over the telephone, enduring the abrupt response of those she calls. The daughter's failure to complete a typewriting course is more than a blow to her self-esteem. Amanda has invested what little money she has to free both herself and Laura.

In this context her son's decision to leave has financial as well as personal implications. He earns a wretched sixty-five dollars a month but in Depression America any job is valuable and, though Tom feels suffocated by work which leaves him little time or space for his poetic ambitions, it has at least served to sustain the family. By leaving he condemns mother and sister to something more than spiritual isolation. The gentleman caller, Jim, meanwhile, recalls visiting the Century of Progress Exposition in Chicago, an exhibition not without its irony in Depression America. . . . To Jim it reveals that the future of America will be "even more wonderful than the present time is!". But we have seen the present, a present in which the Wingfields have been reduced to something approaching a subsistence existence. Indeed Jim's confidence is paper thin for within a few moments he confesses that "I hoped when I was going to high school that I would be further along at this time, six years later, than I am now," his high-school yearbook having predicted inevitable success. If knowledge, money, and power do, indeed, constitute democracy then democracy is itself under threat. And, indeed, Tom is seen, at one stage, reading a newspaper which announces Franco's triumph [Francisco Franco's Fascist forces won the Spanish Civil War], a curious stage direction but one which goes to the heart of Williams's sense of the imperious and implacable power which threatens all his characters.

Materialism Has Failed America

Tom's first speech reiterates that sense of social oppression which Williams had sought to imply through the stage set. "In Spain," he tells us, "there was revolution. Here there was only shouting and confusion. In Spain there was Guernica [a town brutally bombed during the Spanish Civil War]. Here there were disturbances of labor, sometimes pretty violent, in otherwise peaceful cities such as Chicago, Cleveland, Saint Louis." This, he asserts, "is the social background of the play." The middle class of America, he tells us, had "their fingers pressed forcibly down on the fiery Braille alphabet of a dissolving economy." And there is a powerful sense not merely that the animating myths of America have failed those who look for some structure to their lives, but that those myths are themselves the root of a destructive materialism or deceptive illusion.

The play is set at a moment of change, change in the private world of the characters but also in the public world, as though it resonated this private pain. As Tom tells us, "Adventure and change were imminent in this year. They were waiting around the corner for all these kids. Suspended in the mist over Berchtesgarden [site of Adolf Hitler's mountain retreat], caught in the folds of [British prime minister Neville] Chamberlain's umbrella. In Spain there was Guernica! . . . All the world was waiting for bombardments!". It is a speech which does more than situate the play, provide a context for what, by contrast, must seem a minor drama. It is an invitation to read the events ironically, and to see in the desire to live with comforting fictions, rather than confront brutal truths, a doomed and ultimately deadly strategy. For, as Tom indicates in the same speech, whatever consolations or distractions existed—hot swing music, liquor, movies, sex, glass menageries (the last hinted at by his reference to a chandelier)—flooded the world with rainbows which he characterizes as "brief" and "deceptive."

The Wingfields and Society Are Bereft

The Glass Menagerie is more than a lament for a tortured sister (Laura is based on Williams's mentally damaged sister, Rose); it is an elegy for a lost innocence. The Depression had already destroyed one American dream; the war destroyed another, and Tom looks back on the events which he stages in his memory and imagination from the perspective of an immediately postwar world. Neville Chamberlain's piece of paper promising "peace in our time" [the Munich Agreement, which ceded Czechoslovakia to Germany] was no less a product of desperation, no less a symbol of the triumph of hope over despair, than Laura's glass menagerie. Chamberlain's piece of theatre, as he emerged from an aircraft and waved the flag of surrender, believing it to be evidence of his triumph, was no less ironic than Amanda's stage-managed drama of the gentleman caller. In the end brute reality trampled on both.

The Glass Menagerie is no more a play of purely private emotions and concerns than [Anton] Chekhov's *The Cherry Orchard*. In both cases society, no less than the characters who are its expression and in some senses its victims, is caught at a moment of change. Something has broken. We even hear its sound. In Chekhov "A distant sound is heard, coming as if out of the sky, like the sound of a string snapping, slowly and sadly dying away." In *The Glass Menagerie* "There is an ominous cracking sound in the sky ... The sky falls". The snapping of the horn from a glass unicorn thus stands for something more than the end of a private romantic myth. It marks the end of a phase of history, of a particular view of human possibility. . . .

The Play Is Autobiographical

[The play is] rooted firmly in Williams's own life. As he explained, speaking in the year of the play's first production, his family had lived in an apartment not essentially different from that featured in his drama. He recalled his sister's room which was "painted white" with shelves which he had helped her fill "with the little glass animals" which constituted her menagerie. "She was the member of the family with whom I was most in sympathy and, looking back, her glass menagerie had a meaning for me . . . and as I thought about it the glass animals came to represent the fragile, delicate ties that must be broken, that you inevitably break, when you try to fulfill yourself."

This, indeed, is a clue to why Tom, the narrator who shares Tennessee Williams's first name, chooses to "write" the play, in the sense of recalling what seem to him to have been key moments in his past life. For the fact is that the play does have a narrator and his values and perceptions shape the way we see the action, indeed determine what we see. The story is told for a purpose and serves a need outside that story. Tom Wingfield recalls the past for much the same reason that Willy Loman does in [Arthur Miller's] *Death of a Salesman*: guilt. He revisits the past because he knows that his own freedom, such as it is, has been purchased at the price of abandoning others, as Williams had abandoned his mother and, more poignantly, his sister. He "writes" the play, more significantly, perhaps, because he has not effected that escape from the past which had been his primary motive for leaving. The past continues to exert a pull on him, as it does on his mother and sister, as it does on the South which they inhabit.

No Comfort from Past Myths

For his mother, Amanda, the past represents her youth, before time worked its dark alchemy. Memory has become myth, a story to be endlessly repeated as a protection against present decline. She wants nothing more than to freeze time; and in this she mirrors a region whose myths of past grace and romantic fiction mask a sense of present decay. In Williams's words, she clings "frantically to another time and place." The South does no less and Williams (here and in *A Streetcar*

Named Desire), like William Faulkner, acknowledges the seductive yet destructive power of a past reconstituted as myth. At the same time she knows that compromise is necessary. Survival has its price and Amanda is one of Williams's survivors. She survives, ironically, by selling romantic myths, in the form of romance magazines, to other women.

For her daughter, the glass animals of her menagerie transport her into a mythical world, timeless, immune from the onward rush of the twentieth century. It is an immunity, however, which she buys at too high a price for, in stepping into the fictive world of her glass animals, she steps out of any meaningful relationship with others in the present. She becomes one more beautiful but fragile piece in the collection, no longer vulnerable to the depredations of social process or time but no longer redeemed by love.

Tom, meanwhile, prefers the movies, or, more importantly, his poetry. A poet in an unpoetic world, he retreats into his writing because there he can abstract himself from the harsh truths of his existence in a down-at-heel St. Louis apartment. It is not, however, a strategy which has brought him success or peace of mind. He narrates the play in the uniform of the Merchant Marine. He has traded a job in the warehouse for one at sea. There is no suggestion that his desertion of mother and sister has been sanctified by the liberation, or public acknowledgment, of his talent. Like his father before him he has fallen in love with long distance, mistaking movement for progress. Williams himself may have seen Laura's glass animals as representing the fragile, delicate ties that must be broken "when you try to fulfill yourself," but it is clear that in *The Glass Menagerie* Tom has not fulfilled himself. Tennessee Williams may have felt guilty that his success with the play was built on the exploitation of others; Tom lacks even the consolation of success. Fired from his job in the shoe warehouse, he wanders from city to city, looking for the companionship he had failed to offer his sister. In the story version he tells us that he has grown "firm and sufficient." In the play there is no such assurance as, in that Merchant Marine uniform which is the very symbol of his homelessness, he returns, in his memory, to the home he deserted for the fulfillment he failed to find. When his mother asks him to "look out for your sister . . . because she's young and dependent," she identifies an obligation which Tom refuses. In his own life Williams never quite absolved himself of a feeling of guilt with respect to his sister.

Williams Transforms Life into Art

For Tom, memories of the past are a distraction from present failure for though situated in time they exist outside of time. In summoning those memories into existence, he transposes experience into a series of images, transforms life into art, and in so doing mimics the process which his namesake Tom Williams adopts in creating plays, for, as Williams has remarked, the virtue of a play lies in the fact that it occurs "*outside* of time," indeed that it is "*a world without time.*" It is, to his mind, time which renders experience and, indeed, people, inconsequential. Art ascribes meaning to the moment, neutralizes a fear of "*not meaning.*" It is a world in which "emotion and action have a dimension and a dignity that they would . . . have in real existence, if only the shattering intrusion of time could be locked out." The theatrical metaphor, indeed, is central, with Tom as author of a metadrama in which he self-consciously stages his memories as a play in which he performs as narrator. But if he is the primary author, he acknowledges the centrality of Amanda as director, designer, and lighting technician of the drama which has been his life and the life of his tortured sister. . . .

One of the ironies of the play lies in the fact that performance, the imagination's abstraction of the self from its social environment itself, leads into a cul-de-sac not dissimilar to that which lies just beyond the windows of the St. Louis apartment. Tom is fated to restage his drama of the glass menagerie as surely as Ishmael is to recount the story of a white whale [in Herman Melville's *Moby Dick*], as surely as is his sister to dramatize the lives of animals who are touching at least in part because they, like Amanda and Laura in Tom's memory, are unchanging. No matter how many times Tom steps forward to introduce the memories which haunt him, Laura will never escape on the arms of her gentleman caller, nor Amanda redeem her own failed life by finding romance for the daughter she loves but who must always stand as a reproach. . . .

Amanda's Persistence Is Admirable

When Amanda says that "in these trying times we live in, all that we have to cling to is—each other," she voices a conviction which was equally Williams's own, as she does when she observes that "Life's not easy, it calls for—Spartan endurance!" Indeed, though in interviews he often derided his mother, on whom Amanda was modeled, it is clear that it is Amanda who bears the greatest burden, twice abandoned and left to watch over her daughter. Though querulous and puritanical, she is allowed moments of touching vulnerability when she exposes the nature of her own pain ("I've never told you but I—loved your father . . ."). And though she sustains herself with memories and fantasies of a reassuring future, she is forced to an acknowledgment of her situation, as Tom is not. Indeed, Williams himself confessed as much, remarking that, "the mother's valor is the core of *The Glass Menagerie* . . . She's confused, pathetic, even stupid, but everything has got to be all right. She fights to make it that way in the only way she knows how." By necessity she has a practicality which none of the other characters show. At the beginning of the play she proscribes the word "cripple"; at the end she uses the word herself. It is her first step towards accepting the truth of her daughter's situation and hence of the need which she must acknowledge and address.

Williams comments on her cruelty and tenderness, on her derisory yet admirable character, her confused vitality, confused because it appears to lack real purpose. As he remarks in the character notes which precede the play, "she is not paranoiac, but her life is paranoia." The conspiracy of which she is a victim is a fact of existence: youth gives way to age, beauty decays, optimism is subverted by experience, fantasies ground on the rock of the real. She has, he insists, "endurance," but as William Faulkner was to say in his Nobel Prize acceptance speech, endurance is not enough. It is simply the ability to live with irony. He looked, at least in the rhetoric of his speech if not in the action of his novels, for a degree of triumph. There is no real triumph in Williams's plays and precious little in Faulkner's novels. What there is is "a kind of heroism," and that is precisely the quality which he has ascribed to Amanda. Deserted and betrayed, she stays and continues her losing battle with time in the company of her doomed daughter and, in what is virtually the play's final stage direction, Williams finds a "dignity and tragic beauty" in that sad alliance. It is no longer the absurdity of this abandoned woman he chooses to stress. At the beginning of the play he had described her expression as "grim and hopeless." She shakes her head in despair, having just learned of her daughter's deception in abandoning her typing course. At the end we are told that her "gestures are slow and graceful, almost dancelike," as she comforts that same daughter.

Early in the play we are told that her face has "aged but childish features," that it is "cruelly sharp, satirical as a [Honoré] Daumier print." At the end, with her words inaudible to us, she is once more presented to us in visual terms in a kind of *tableau vivant* [living picture]. This time, though, it is an image drained of irony. What communicates is less cruelty than charity, less sharpness than a soft maternal attentiveness. At least in memory Tom embraces the woman he has otherwise blamed for his own problems, for the suffocating years in the shoe warehouse and for the guilt which has made him return, in memory, to St. Louis where he had abandoned her and failed to redeem his sister from her isolation.

In a world "lit by lightning," Laura's candles cast a softer glow. In the end the lightning will prevail, at least in the short term. Art can never really be a protection against the real. Chamberlain's betrayals, Franco's victories, Hitler's barbarity were not defeated by wishing they might be so, and, as [Anglo-American poet W.H.] Auden lamented, poetry did not save a single Jew [from the Holocaust]. Williams was acutely aware of this. Why else have Tom open the play with a reminder of what lay in wait for those caught in the Depression and consoling themselves with movies, glamor magazines and dance music entitled, "The World is Waiting for the Sunrise"? At the same time he was wedded to art, whose power does indeed lie in its ability to outlive even the traumas of history. He was wedded to theatre whose form and whose substance exposed the nature of the paradox, as it offers truth through lies and reveals a tensile strength in the most fragile of creations.

The Glass Menagerie Depicts the Destruction of a Family

Benjamin Nelson

An adjunct professor of English at Fairleigh Dickinson University in New Jersey, Benjamin Nelson is the author of Arthur Miller: Portrait of a Playwright.

The central character in The Glass Menagerie *is Amanda, asserts Nelson in the following selection. Although she is ultimately defeated, she puts up a valiant fight for a better life for her children, Nelson points out. Her children are also defeated—Tom takes no joy in deserting his mother and sister, and Laura copes with her disappointment by retreating further into a world of fantasy, he explains. The Wingfields are doomed—both individually and as a family, Nelson declares.*

In *The Glass Menagerie* the [D.H.] Lawrence influence . . . seems to be present in the story of a son's need to break away from his mother and the awakening of a repressed female by a vital male. But to belabor these similarities any further than the mention of them would be unfair to Tennessee Williams and to his play. *The Glass Menagerie* is the most consciously biographical of all Williams' dramas, and if the seven scenes which comprise this play are not literal representations of the St. Louis days in the early 1930s they nevertheless blend into an uncompromising emotional portrait of the tragic situation which was the author's home.

Amanda's Futile Hopes

The story is simple. Tom Wingfield, a young man with dreams, is bound to his mother and sister because his father vanished one day and left them destitute. He realizes how much he is

Benjamin Nelson, "The Play Is Memory," in *Tennessee Williams: The Man and His Work*. New York: Ivan Obolensky, 1961, pp. 97–112.

needed, and yet he knows that he must escape from them if he is ever to find himself. "His nature is not remorseless, but to escape from a trap he has to act without pity." The mother, Amanda, lives in two worlds: the pleasant dream of the past, Moon Lake Casino, Blue Mountain, the memory of seventeen gentleman callers in a single day, and the drab and demanding world of the present, with bills to pay, a son who is "a poet with a job in a warehouse," and a daughter who has refused to accept the harsh reality of her life and has withdrawn into the world of glass figurines she has collected "till she is like a piece of her own glass collection, too exquisitely fragile to move from the shelf." Concerned about her son, whom she does not understand, and who she feels must gather himself together and face his responsibilities, Amanda is much more distraught with her daughter who, she realizes, is helpless and lost. An attempt to instill confidence in her by sending her to secretarial school has been a dismal failure, and Amanda has only one last hope: to find a husband who will provide for her and somehow keep her from submerging entirely into a world of imagination.

At his mother's almost cajoling insistence, Tom finally brings home a gentleman caller, a young man named Jim O'Connor who works with him at the shoe corporation. The final two scenes of the play present the supper at the Wingfield home and the incipient relationship between Jim and Laura. For a brief, breathless moment Laura emerges from the glass menagerie, but while she is still swaying precariously on the threshold, Jim admits that he is already keeping company and is soon going to be married. As the world crashes, he departs, Amanda berates Tom for his apparent stupidity and then hastens to comfort her daughter who has finally enclosed herself in her illusions. And Tom Wingfield now breaks free and departs into the world from which Laura has made her final, irrevocable retreat. . . .

Amanda Is Heroic

The story of Laura and Jim is simple and poignant, but it is neither the sole nor the central conflict in the play. Laura's personal dilemma is part of a greater dilemma: the destruction—slow and remorseless—of a family. It is not a melodramatic destruction; there is no battle of angels above them. It is gradual, oblique and laced with pathos and humor, but it is the erosion of a family nonetheless; and the central protagonist of this drama is not Laura, but Amanda, her mother. Amanda Wingfield is [as Williams directs in his character notes:]

> a little woman of great but confused vitality clinging frantically to another time and place. Her characterization must be carefully created, not copied from type. She is not paranoiac, but her life is paranoia. There is much to admire in Amanda, and as much to love and pity as there is to laugh at. Certainly she has endurance and a kind of heroism, and though her foolishness makes her unwittingly cruel at times, there is tenderness in her slight person.

Amanda does cling frantically to the past, but she clings just as desperately to the present. She is attempting to hold two worlds together and realizes that both are crumbling beneath her fingers. The world of her youth has already vanished and her constant references to gentleman callers and jonquils are not only out of place in the dingy St. Louis apartment—they are agonizing. Her horribly dated clothing and her mannerisms also underscore her as a foolish old woman impossibly attempting to relive a wasted life. Puritanical and narrow minded, she is appalling in her unreasonable devotion to the past. At the same time she is shrewish, nagging and vulgar in her attempts to cope with the bleak reality of her environment. At one moment she enrages her son with her pretentions and her postures, in the next she prods him and goads him for his inability to be more than a dreamer in a situation where positive action is needed. She berates Tom with the statement that

> you are the only young man that I know who ignores the fact that the future becomes the present, the present the past, and the past turns into everlasting regret if you don't plan for it.

Amanda does not ignore these facts. She recognizes them all too well and attempts to flaunt them with her own special dreams. She knows that her existence and the existence of her son and daughter is a desperate struggle, and she accepts that struggle. It is this acceptance which elevates her stature above the cloying, often ignorant and embarrassing dowdy, and makes her the most vital and moving character in the play. For whatever Amanda is or does, she possesses a fighting spirit and a stubborn gallantry in the face of overwhelming odds. And in Williams' words, "the most magnificent thing in all human nature is valor—and endurance." It is precisely this heroism and endurance which finally manifest themselves in Amanda and leave us with the impression of a truly valiant woman. This impression does not arise out of any particular word or action. Throughout the play she nags, scolds, dreams, plays the coquette and rages helplessly at her son. And yet, although nothing is said in her behalf, she emerges as a noble and strangely tender figure with a valor that abides alongside pettiness and a tenderness which is at once intertwined with insensitivity and cruelty. It is only at the conclusion when she realizes that her desperate plan for Laura has been crushingly defeated that the great strength and beauty of this woman emerges.

> The interior scene is played as though viewed through soundproof glass. Amanda appears to be making a comforting speech to Laura who is huddled upon the sofa. Now that we cannot hear the mother's voice, her silliness is gone

and she has dignity and tragic beauty. Laura's dark hair hides her face until at the end of the speech she lifts it to smile at her mother.

Williams' portrait of Amanda is one of the most compelling and honest he has ever drawn. If it is not a factual likeness of the playwright's mother—he reports that she was aghast when she first viewed Laurette Taylor's performance—it is nevertheless an unerring emotional portrait drawn with amazing candor and with great objectivity. And the ambivalence in the relationship between the son and the mother is as poignant as it is terrifying.

In his story of the disintegration of a family and the desperate need for one member of that family to break free, Williams has presented a deeply moving play. For Amanda, as for Laura, and even for Jim to a lesser extent, life is finally overwhelming. Despite their gallantry, bluster, tenderness and rage, they are defeated. . . .

No Success in Tom's Escape

Tom Wingfield, the son and narrator . . . is caught in the web of his family and is fully aware of his plight. He knows that his job in the shoe company will stifle him and the anguish he feels in the presence of his mother will soon tear him apart. He knows that one day he will have to commit the cruelest act of his life: abandoning mother and sister. As [critic John] Gassner noted, he may love and sympathize with these people but he cannot accept their failure. The world will not accept them and Tom must make his stand in the world, "for nowadays the world is lit by lightning. Blow out your candles, Laura—and so good bye. . . ." So Tom leaves "with a wide-awake attitude toward a society that . . . challenges our intelligence and capacity for action." He cuts the silver cord and like Paul Morel of [D.H. Lawrence's novel] *Sons and Lovers* walks out of the darkness toward the challenging and shimmering unknown.

But is Tom Wingfield's departure a positive effort on his part, or the final fraying of a bond which could no longer maintain itself? Tom, in the role of Narrator, speaks a good deal about truth and illusion and reality and dreams, but Tom, the protagonist in the story, possesses the romantic soul of a dreamer. Despite the perceptions he shows as Narrator he has as much trouble facing his situation as does his mother. In part, the play is his attempt to overcome his fears, but we are left with no assurance at the conclusion that he has succeeded. He is plainly disgusted with his mother for her poses and apparent refusal to cope with reality, and yet he, too, escapes daily from the oppression of his life by seeking the narcotism of the cinema. Before he makes his final departure Amanda accuses him of living in illusions:

> Go to the movies, go! Don't think about us, a mother deserted, an unmarried sister who's crippled and has no job! Don't let anything interfere with your selfish pleasure! Just go, go, go—to the movies!

Thus a mother who is accused by her son of living in illusions, makes the most harsh and realistic statement in the play when she berates the boy, who considers himself the realist, for being an ineffectual dreamer. The author of the play is here not the narrator. Williams turns a double-edged blade unmercifully, honestly and beautifully. When Tom leaves he escapes from a trap, a situation which is plainly unendurable, but there is nothing heroic or even positive and challenging in his departure. He is discharged from his position with the shoe company and he knows he can no longer remain home. His departure is little more than the snap of a twig in the wind.

Tom is a part of the dilemma of his family and he cannot break completely free. If the bond between him and his mother and sister has frayed, it nevertheless holds and will hold all his life. As he admits in retrospect, "Oh Laura, Laura,

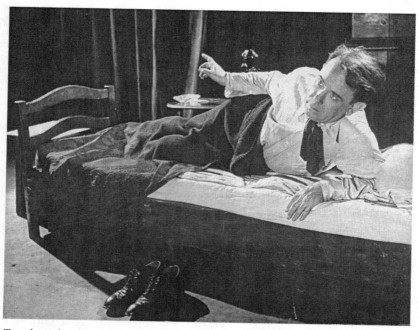

Tom, here played by Eddie Dowling in the original 1945 Broadway production, knows his life and family situation are untenable but he cannot fully break away from his mother and sister. © George Karger/Time & Life Pictures/Getty Images.

I tried to leave you behind me, but I am more faithful than I intended to be." Wherever he may go and whatever he may do, he will always be more faithful than he intended to be, to Amanda as well as Laura. In the final analysis, he is the fourth of a quartet caught in the ordinary and terrifying situation of attempting to exist in a world which gives them no sensible reason for existence. . . .

All the Characters Are Failures

But the great weakness of *The Glass Menagerie* does not lie in its author's artistic or technical deficiencies. The weakness lies at the core of the play and evolves out of what is to become the playwright's hardening philosophical commitment. We can begin to comprehend this when we ask ourselves whether or not *The Glass Menagerie* is a tragedy. It presents a tragic situation and characters who, despite their moodiness and foolishness and self-deception, possess a sense of the tragic. With the possible exception of Laura, they are intensely genuine and the destruction of their dreams and aspirations bears the illusion of great importance. But the play is not a tragedy. The universe of *The Glass Menagerie* does not allow tragedy.

Everyone in the play is a failure and in the course of their drama they all perish a little. Amanda, the most heroic of the quartet, is pitiful but not tragic because from the outset she is doomed to failure despite her desperate struggle to right things. None of these people are given the opportunity to triumph against a fate which is as malignant as it is implacable. Their struggle is a rear-guard action against life, a continuous retreat. This retreat may be moving, pathetic, melodramatic or boisterous, but it is always a withdrawal. After all, what is the world outside the glass menagerie?

> There was only hot swing music and liquor, dance halls, bars and movies, and sex that hung in the gloom like a chandelier and flooded the world with brief, deceptive rainbows . . . all the world was waiting for bombardments!

The world outside the Wingfield apartment is a world of illusions, also, even more deceptive and destructive than those held by Amanda and Laura. It is the world of [Williams's early play] *Stairs to the Roof* and this time the escape is not to a new star but into the individual and personal illusions fostered by each of the characters as his private defense against destruction. Jim waits for the day when his "zzzzzp!" will at last disperse his fear and uncertainty: Laura creates her own sparkling, cold world which gives the illusion of warmth but is as eternal in its unreality as the glass from which it is composed; Amanda strikes out with all her power against her fate by clinging to the past as to a shield; and Tom, recognizing the plight of his family, can do no more than drift away from them, rudderless, frightened and never really as far from Amanda and Laura as he knows he should be.

Not one of these individuals can cope with his situation. They struggle and their hopes and the destruction of these hopes possess a sense of great importance because Williams has created genuine people in an intensely genuine situation, but they lack the completeness to truly cope with their dilemma. They are not responsible for what has happened to them and they are much too helpless to do more than delay the inevitable. And destruction is inevitable because it is implicit in the universe of Tennessee Williams.

> For the sins of the world are really only its partialities, and these are what sufferings must atone for.... The nature of man is full of such makeshift arrangements, devised by himself to cover his incompletion. He feels a part of himself to be like a missing wall or a room left unfurnished and he tries as well as he can to make up for it. The use of imagination, resorting to dreams or the loftier purpose of art, is a mask he devises to cover his incompletion. Or violence such as a war, between two men or among a number of nations, is also a blind and senseless compensation for that which is not yet formed in human nature. Then there is still another compensation. This one is found in the principle of atonement, the surrender of self to violent treatment by others with the idea of thereby cleansing one's self of his guilt.

This statement emanates from the core of Williams' thought and is perhaps his most illuminating commentary about himself and his work. It represents a philosophy, or let us say an attitude toward man in his universe, which is to manifest itself in all his work....

The underlying belief in *The Glass Menagerie* is that there is very little, if any, reason for living. Man is by nature incomplete because his universe is fragmented. There is nothing to be done about this condition because nothing *can* be done about it. Human guilt becomes a corollary of universal guilt and man's life is an atonement for the human condition. In each character in *The Glass Menagerie* there is a part "like a missing wall or a room left unfurnished and he tries as well as he can to make up for it." The mask devised by Laura and Amanda and Tom and Jim is "the use of imagination, resorting to dreams." The Wingfields are broken, fragmented people because "the sins of the world are really only its partialities." They are really not at all responsible for their condition, and thus are in no way able to cope with it. They are trapped in a determined universe. Without some kind of responsibility on the part of the protagonist there is opportunity neither for tragic elevation nor tragic fall. The Wingfields were doomed the moment they were born. At best their struggles will allow them to survive ... for a time. They will never be allowed to triumph. Thus their struggles, their hopes and even their eventual destruction can never move far beyond pathos. The beauty and magic of *The Glass Menagerie* is that this pathos is genuine, objective and deeply moving.

Williams Uses Mirrors to Depict Family Dysfunction

Eric P. Levy

Eric P. Levy is associate professor of English at the University of British Columbia. He is the author of several books on drama, including Hamlet and the Rethinking of Man.

Williams uses mirrors in The Glass Menagerie *to symbolize self-consciousness and fragile self-image, Levy suggests in the following essay. As an example, he cites how Amanda asks Laura to look in the mirror, then destroys her daughter's self-confidence by flattering herself at her daughter's expense. Mirrors are also used to symbolize the way in which Jim destroys Laura's brittle self-esteem, Levy relates. Continually looking in the mirror to admire himself, Jim is concerned only with his self-image and has little concern for the devastating impact his actions have on Laura, Levy explains.*

In his production notes introducing *The Glass Menagerie,* Tennessee Williams refers to nostalgia as "the first condition of the play." This appraisal at first seems accurate, for the drama disposes the past in a series of receding planes by which the very notion of nostalgia is progressively deepened. From the perspective of Tom, the narrator and a chief character, the past when he started "to boil inside" with the urge to leave home becomes a haunting memory from which his present struggles vainly to flee. But the confining power of that past derives from his mother's nostalgic attachment to her own more distant past and the desperate need to exploit motherhood as a means of reviving *"the legend of her youth."*

Eric P. Levy, "Through Soundproof Glass: The Prison of Self-Consciousness in *The Glass Menagerie," Modern Drama,* vol. 36, no. 4, December 1993, pp. 529–37. Copyright © 1993 by Modern Drama. All rights reserved. Reproduced by permission.

Yet once we analyse how Amanda manipulates maternity, a factor in the play more fundamental than nostalgia will begin to emerge. This principle is self-consciousness—a term which, as we shall see, the text supplies and in its own way defines. Each character is hampered in relating to others by the need to inhabit a private world where the fundamental concern is with self-image. Some characters (Amanda and Jim) use others as mirrors to reflect the self-image with which they themselves wish to identify. Other characters (Laura and Tom) fear that through relation to others they will be reduced to mere reflections, trapped in the mirror of the other's judgment. In virtue of this preoccupation with self-image and the psychological mirrors sustaining it, the world of the play is aptly named after glass. Indeed, Laura's remark ironically becomes the motto of the play: "My glass collection takes up a good deal of time. Glass is something you have to take good care of."

Let us begin by examining Amanda's influence on Laura. Unwittingly, Amanda exploits her maternal concern about Laura's lack of marital prospects as a means of identifying with her own past when she herself was visited one Sunday afternoon in Blue Mountain by "seventeen!—gentlemen callers." In effect, she turns her daughter into a mirror in which her own flattering self-image is reflected, but to do so she must first turn herself or, more precisely, her parental judgment, into a mirror reflecting Laura's limitations. The play itself suggests this seminal image. After helping Laura dress and groom herself, Amanda instructs her to stand in front of a real mirror: "Now look at yourself, young lady. This is the prettiest you will ever be!—I've got to fix myself now! You're going to be surprised by your mother's appearance!" Then *"Laura moves slowly to the long mirror and stares solemnly at herself."*

In this essay, Levy analyzes how mirrors are used in The Glass Menagerie. *Here, Amanda, played by actress Jessica Lange in a 2007 stage production, moves in front of a mirror.* © Geraint Lewis/Alamy.

Laura Is Put Down by Amanda

Look closely at what is happening here. Amanda slights Laura's appearance even as she praises it. Laura is told that she has reached her peak at this moment: she will never again be as attractive. But Laura's limitation only enhances Amanda's excitement about her own "spectacular appearance!". The literal mirror in which Laura beholds her own image ultimately symbolizes her mother's judgment of her. Yet the fundamental purpose of that judgment is to provide, by contrast, a flattering self-image for Amanda. Though on this occasion Amanda's judgment seems benign, it participates in a subtle pattern of comparison by which Laura is made to identify with the sense of her own "Inferiority" to her mother. Indeed, at one point she alludes explicitly to this fact: "I'm just not popular like you were in Blue Mountain." Laura is, in her own words, "crippled." But her primary handicap concerns, not the limp caused by a slight inequality in the length of her legs, but the negative self-consciousness instilled by her mother. In fact Jim, the gentleman caller, approaches this very diagnosis. When Laura recalls how in high school she "had to go clumping all the way up the aisle with everyone watching," Jim advises: "You shouldn't have been self-conscious."

The effect of Laura's self-consciousness is to make her intensely protective of her self-image, and to shield it from exposure to anyone outside the home. Whenever she is forced to interact or perform in public, she becomes suddenly ill with nausea and must withdraw. The most extreme example of this syndrome is her brief attendance at Rubicam's Business College where, according to the typing instructor, Laura "broke down completely—was sick at the stomach and almost had to be carried into the wash room". She has a similar reaction after the arrival of Jim at the Wingfield home, and reclines alone on her couch while the others dine in another room. As a result of this withdrawal reflex, Laura has no life outside preoccupation with her own vulnerability.

But paradoxically, the very intensity of this preoccupation changes the meaning of the vulnerability it concerns. By focusing on the fear of humiliating exposure, Laura eventually identifies, not with the shame evoked by her self-image, but with the desperate need to avoid suffering it. In this context, the playwright's commentary on Laura gains greater profundity: "Laura's separation increases till she is like a piece of her own glass collection, too exquisitely fragile to move from the shelf." At bottom, the purpose of Laura's withdrawal *is* to heighten her "fragility"; for, through belief in the damaging effect of exposure, she exchanges a negative self-image for one more flattering. Sensitivity to shame allows Laura to identify with her worthiness, not of ridicule, but of delicate care and compassion. Yet instead of leading to "confidence," this escape from shame depends on increasing her insecurity. She is safe from exposure to shame only if she identifies with her inability to endure it. But lack of confidence is Laura's secret wish, for it protects from confronting anything more threatening in life than her own familiar anxiety. Indeed, whenever she is encouraged to go beyond this anxiety, her reflex is to pick up one of her "little glass ornaments." She does this when Amanda reminds her of the need for eventual marriage and during the conversation with Jim.

The Menagerie as Laura's Self-Image

The significance of these ornaments can be clarified by closer consideration of the glass from which they are made. In the play, glass is associated not just with the "lovely fragility" already noted, but also with the mirror prominently visible in the Wingfield apartment. Earlier we encountered one example where Amanda instructs Laura to observe her reflection in the mirror, but we shall examine several other allusions to this literal mirror; it becomes a vital symbol of the act of self-consciousness by which a character apprehends his or her self-image. Yet, in Laura's case, this analogy between the literal mirror and the act of self-consciousness extends further. Just as with a real mirror the reflection perceived is an image in glass, so in the play, as we have seen, Laura's own self-image is represented by ornaments of glass. Hence, in virtue of the glass which is their substance, these ornaments suggest that the fragility with which she identifies is no more than a self-image, dependent on the mirror of self-consciousness reflecting it.

But whereas Laura's recourse is to emphasize the mirror of negative self-consciousness, Tom's impulse is to shatter it, in order thereby to achieve his freedom. Like Laura, he too is exposed to the mirror of parental judgment held up by his mother, Amanda. But, unlike his sister, Tom refuses to identify with the negative self-image it reflects. His consuming wish is to leave home and explore his manhood: "I'm tired of the *movies*, and I am *about* to *move!*". But Amanda insists that his desire to leave home is simply a manifestation of selfishness, and further proof that he will end up as faithless and irresponsible as his father, an example of the kind of man he should never become. In fact, a photograph of that father, hanging "*on the wall of the living room*", functions as a kind of mirror displaying the very self-image with which Tom is identified: "More and more you remind me of your father! He was out all hours without explanation!—Then *left! Goodbye!* And me with the bag to hold." Yet, with increasing passion, Tom protests his right to be a person and not merely a reflection defined by his mother's way of seeing him. Ultimately, he refuses to let the image she holds up to him restrain him; for if he identifies with it, he will never be free.

Breaking Glass as Liberation

The process of this repudiation is repeatedly linked with the breakage of glass, symbol of the reflected self-image with which a character is made to identify. In the first great confrontation with his mother, Tom disowns the self-image with which she tries to control him: "For sixty-five dollars a month I give up all that I dream of doing and being *ever!* And you say self—*self's* all I ever think of. Why, listen, if self is what I thought of, Mother, I'd be where he is—GONE!". Then, in an enraged effort to don his overcoat and leave the house, he becomes entangled in *"the bulky garment"* and heaves it *"across the room."* The result is devastating: *"It strikes against the shelf of Laura's glass collection, and there is a tinkle of shattering glass. Laura cries out as if wounded."* On the surface, Tom's fury here seems purely destructive, damaging the possession which his sister most prizes. But, more profoundly, Tom's action represents the only way of claiming his own identity. If he allows his mother to restrain him by guilt and convince him that to act on his own is to become like his father, he will be no more self-reliant than Laura, hampered in life by a negative self-image, symbolized in Laura's case by the glass menagerie. For Laura, that self-image concerns fragility; for Tom, guilt. But each image is equally restricting.

Tom's second confrontation with his mother is even more explosive. Once again, she imposes a negative image upon him: "Go to the movies, go! Don't think about us, a mother deserted, an unmarried sister who's crippled and has no job! Don't let anything interfere with your selfish pleasure!". In rage, *"Tom smashes his glass on the floor"* and then *"plunges out on the fire escape, slamming the door."* The act of breaking glass (in this instance, a drinking vessel) obviously recalls the earlier shattering of an item in Laura's glass menagerie. Again, in the struggle to affirm and fulfil his own identity, Tom is forced to repudiate the negative image reflected in the mirror of parental judgment. What he says in the first encounter also explains his reaction in the second: "It seems unimportant to you, what I'm *doing*—what I *want* to do."

Seeking to Escape Amanda's Judgment

But even after leaving the house to explore life on his own, Tom is still haunted by the mirror of parental judgment. His *"closing speech"*, immediately after the second glass-smashing episode, is extremely revealing in this regard. In describing his itinerant life after breaking away from home, Tom admits that, at bottom, his freedom is no more than a flight in which he feels "pursued by something" that turns out to be the image of his sister. He recounts an obsession that overwhelms him each time he arrives in a new town: "Perhaps I am walking along a street at night, in some strange city, before I have found companions. I pass the lighted window of a shop where perfume is sold. The window is filled with pieces of colored glass, tiny transparent bottles in delicate colors, like bits of a shattered rainbow. Then all at once my sister touches my shoulder. I turn around and look in to her eyes."

This is one of the most poignant passages in the play, but understanding its full meaning requires some analysis. On the surface, Tom seems obsessed with guilt for having abandoned the sister who depended on him. But his preoccupation with Laura involves much more than the sense of duty denied. Or, more precisely, his remorse is motivated by a concern deeper than shirked obligation. The context confirms this. Her apparition usually appears after Tom sees some "tiny transparent bottles" through a shop window. The delicate ornaments, of course, remind him of Laura's glass menagerie. Ironically, however, in his futile flight from the memory of Laura, he is trying to escape an insecurity analogous to one symbolized by that glass menagerie. Whereas Laura reacts to insecurity by withdrawing into "a world of her own—a world of little glass ornaments," Tom responds by plunging compulsively into a world of strangers: "I cross the street, I run into the movies or a bar, I buy a drink, I speak to the nearest stranger—anything that can blow your candles out!" In fact, in his restless flight after leaving home, when cities whirl past him "like dead leaves," Tom travels perpetually through a world of strangers, never staying still long enough to find a new place he can call home.

The nature of this insecurity becomes clearer when we consider the scene with which its description is synchronized. As the author notes, "*Tom's closing speech is timed with what is happening inside the house. We see, as though through sound-*

proof glass, that Amanda appears to be making a comforting speech to Laura, who is huddled upon the sofa." The emphasis on *"soundproof glass"* is crucial here. To live in that home *is* to live behind a pane of imaginary glass: namely, the mirror of parental judgment created by Amanda in order to flatter her own self-image. To live inside that home is to be defined by the mirror it contains, as we have seen extensively with regard to Laura and Tom. Now that he is outside the home, Tom can see through that soundproof glass, as if it were a one-way mirror, transparent to the viewer or audience on one side, but a reflecting surface to those trapped on the other side of it.

Both Tom and Laura Are Prisoners

The great pathos of the play is that Tom remains just as much a prisoner of the mirror as Laura. His attempt to flee merely confirms its influence. The ultimate cause of his restless movement is the fear of finding himself trapped on the wrong side of the mirror again—in other words, enclosed in an intimacy founded on love. For to love, as Tom has learned through the relation with his mother, is to be exposed to a mirror of negative judgment on which one becomes dependent for the sense of one's own worth. In that position, Tom is as vulnerable to insecurity as Laura. Hence, though his need for companionship is great, his need for loneliness is greater; for only loneliness can protect him from the vulnerability to love (or, more precisely, to the mirror of judgment which love creates) epitomized by his sister. But paradoxically, by shielding him from the same vulnerability to love suffered by Laura, loneliness increases his identification with her; for in that state he inhabits a world of his own, just as she does through preoccupation with the glass menagerie. The instability of this condition is vividly represented by Tom's obsession with Laura. Her image always appears in his moments of greatest loneliness—when he has just entered a new town at night but has not yet "found companions." He recoils from her and compulsively seeks strangers, but soon after meeting them he is once again on his lonely way. Thus the cycle of his life continues.

Jim Motivated by Self-Interest

An even more profound pessimism about the influence of the mirror emerges when we examine Jim, the gentleman caller, who, according to Tom, "is the most realistic character in the play, being an emissary from a world of reality that we were somehow set apart from." It soon becomes apparent, however, that Jim is as much defined by mirrors and the self-consciousness which they symbolize as anyone else in the drama. Jim does show a genuine interest in Laura and tries to help her: "You don't have the proper amount of faith in yourself." Nevertheless, his concern is tainted with self-interest. Ultimately, like Amanda, he exploits Laura as a mirror in which to reflect a flattering image of himself.

The play is explicit in this regard. Note how, when encouraging Laura to conquer her "Inferiority complex," Jim "*unconsciously glances at himself in the mirror*" as he tells her that "Everybody excels in some one thing. Some in many!". A moment later, he "*adjusts his tie at the mirror.*" In effect, he uses her need for self-confidence as an opportunity to admire his own attributes: "I guess you think I think a lot of myself!" His parting gesture sums up the meaning of his interest in Laura: "*He stops at the oval mirror to put on his hat. He carefully shapes the brim and the crown to give a discreetly dashing effect.*" While Jim's reunion with Laura has aroused sincere affection for her, his deepest love is reserved for his own self-image. Consistently, he uses her sense of inadequacy as a means of magnifying his own positive attributes: "Look how big my shadow is when I stretch!" At bottom, what appears to be compassion—and what to Jim feels like honest compassion—is nothing more than narcissism, where awareness of Laura's emotional need leaves Jim "*enrapt in his own comfortable being.*" This selfishness is most apparent when he kisses her. Jim yields to his attraction to Laura, but in doing so reveals its deepest motive. As soon as he kisses her he must reject her, because he already has a girlfriend, Betty. His sudden reversal makes Laura suffer an *"almost infinite desolation,"* but reinforces Jim's own complacent satisfaction with himself: "Being in love has made a new man of me!" Once again, he turns Laura's helplessness into a mirror in which his own self-assurance is reflected.

Laura's situation is made more devastating by the positive effect he initially has on her. When the unicorn's horn breaks during her brief dance with Jim, Laura is not upset: "It's no tragedy, Freckles. Glass breaks so easily." In fact, she seems on the brink of transcending the image of herself which the unicorn represents: "The horn was removed to make him feel less—freakish!" Before he leaves, Laura gives Jim the unicorn as a "souvenir," then *"rises unsteadily and crouches beside the Victrola to wind it up."* These gestures are supremely significant. Giving away the unicorn suggests that the release from negative self-consciousness with which she has just identified the ornament in its newly damaged state has already ended. This suggestion is corroborated by the movement which follows her surrender of the unicorn: winding up the gramophone. Earlier, in a passage we have already quoted, Tom connected Laura's preoccupation with the Victrola with her withdrawal from reality: "She lives in a world of her own—a world of little glass ornaments, Mother. [. . .] She plays old phonograph records and—that's about all."

Laura's offering of the unicorn has further implications. For, through preoccupation with his own self-image, Jim—like Laura—inhabits a world of his own which no true intimacy can violate. The only difference is that, while Laura identifies as the victim of self-consciousness, Jim identifies as its beneficiary. The fundamental function of his love for another is to enhance his love for himself.

Williams's Major Theme Is the Destructive Impact of Society on the Sensitive Individual

Nancy M. Tischler

Nancy M. Tischler is professor emerita of English and the humanities at Pennsylvania State University and the author of Black Masks: Negro Characters in Modern Southern Fiction.

According to Tischler in the following selection, each of the Wingfields has difficulty adapting to a modern, industrialized, northern existence. Amanda remembers wistfully the days when she was a sought-after southern belle, Tom is a poet trapped in a soulless factory job, and Laura is overwhelmed by her physical defect, Tischler relates. Jim represents the real world—a world that the Wingfields can only futilely hope to join.

The mother Williams had chosen to write about in *The Glass Menagerie* was, naturally, his own. The story is that of his last years in St. Louis—the Depression, "when the huge middle class of America was matriculating in a school for the blind. Their eyes had failed them, or they had failed their eyes, and so they were having their fingers pressed forcibly down on the fiery Braille alphabet of a dissolving economy." Tom, the hero, is working days at the shoe factory and writing nights in his stuffy room or going to the movies. The father of the play, who deserted the family some years earlier, having been a telephone man who fell in love with long distances, haunts the scene pleasantly in the form of an ineluctably smiling photograph. The mother, Amanda Wingfield, is trying to

Nancy M. Tischler, "The Glass Menagerie," in *Tennessee Williams: Rebellious Puritan.* New York: The Citadel Press, 1961, pp. 91–116. Copyright © 1961 by Nancy M. Tischler. All rights reserved. Reproduced by permission.

hold the family together and to steer her children into more practical paths than those she has followed herself, for she is a disillusioned romantic turned evangelical realist.

Trying to Find Laura a Husband

She lectures Tom on the merits of tending to business. By soliciting magazine subscriptions over the phone she finances a secretarial course in business school for Laura, her daughter. When Amanda finds that Laura is too nervous to learn to type, she decides that the girl must marry. This requires exposing her to an eligible bachelor, whom, to his consternation, Tom is to provide. Tom finally approaches Jim O'Connor, a fellow employee at the shoe factory, and invites him to dinner. Overdoing it, as usual, Amanda sets about redecorating the house and revising her daughter's dress and personality. Her frenzy makes the trio increasingly tense as they await the approach of Jim, the gentleman caller.

Jim had known Laura in high school and has been her idol for years. His nice manners appeal to Amanda. The dinner, consequently, proceeds beautifully, with only one slight interruption: the lights go off because Tom has spent the electric-bill money. Candlelight, however, suffices.

After dinner, Amanda hauls her son to the kitchen to provide privacy to the young couple whom this obvious maneuver reduces to painful embarrassment. Very shortly, though, Jim's good nature melts Laura's shyness, and she finds herself sitting on the floor with him chatting cozily by candlelight, sipping dandelion wine. They talk of Jim's ambitions in electro-dynamics and of his night-school courses. Then they turn to a discussion of Laura's collection of tiny glass animals and of her prize, a little unicorn. When, a few minutes later, they start to dance, Jim stumbles and breaks the horn off the little animal. Laura cradles her pet in her palm, musing that he is better off without his horn, for now he can be normal, like the other animals of the menagerie.

In this glimpse, we realize that sweet, simple Laura believes in these little creatures with the same eagerness that Jim believes in electro-dynamics. Finally, in a clumsy effort to apply his half-digested understanding of psychology, Jim decides that Laura has an inferiority complex and that he can cure it with a kiss. Then, horrified at what his action might suggest to this fuzzily romantic girl, he blurts out the secret that he is engaged. Laura, strangely enough, seems to be no more hurt by this clumsiness than by the breaking of the unicorn. Rather, on learning that her gentleman caller is not an eligible bachelor, she smiles stoically and gives him her now-hornless unicorn as a souvenir.

The tender mood is broken by the gay entrance of Amanda, bearing a pitcher of lemonade and singing a cruelly appropriate song about lemonade and old maids. Jim, finally understanding why he was invited, takes this moment to explain to Amanda that he plans to marry soon. Then he beats a hasty retreat. Amanda turns spittingly upon her son, who in turn stalks off to the movies. She screams after him that he can "go to the moon" since he is nothing but a selfish dreamer anyway. The final scene is a *tableau vivant* ["living picture"] of Amanda, looking dignified and beautiful, comforting her daughter while Tom explains that he eventually escaped from the women to follow the pattern of his roving father. This simple story, turning on a dinner party given by a Southern family for an outsider whom they hope to match with their unmarried daughter and the character revelations that occur in its course, constitutes Tennessee Williams' most fragile and lovely play.

Tom Longs to Escape a Dreary Life

In some ways, *The Glass Menagerie* is a variation of the battle-of-angels theme. Tom expresses the same need to escape the nailed-up coffin of his restricted existence that Val expresses in the earlier play [*Battle of Angels*, which Williams described

133

as "a prayer for the Wild at Heart Kept in Cages"]; but Tom seems to be more conscious of a corresponding loss that such freedom implies. He rejects the possessive love of his family because he can accept it only by shouldering the responsibility and accepting the imprisonment that go with it. The rejection of this relationship gives him pain, however, as his proposed desertion of Myra apparently did not give Val. This is a more realistic evaluation of human needs and yearnings. The characters also are more realistic. Although Tom and the others in *The Glass Menagerie* may represent attitudes toward life, none are personified abstractions. There is no Jabe to represent death. A subtler type of characterization combined with a simpler, less melodramatic story yields a far more artistic product.

One of the chief characters is sketched only by implication. The father of the Wingfield family hovers over the scene, although he never appears on stage at all. An enlarged photograph of him, which the spotlight occasionally illuminates, reminds us of his part in the formation of the dramatic situation. It is the picture of a handsome young man in a doughboy's cap. Though deeply hurt by his desertion, Amanda considers her erstwhile husband the embodiment of romance, associating him with that time in her life when the house in Blue Mountain was filled with gentleman callers and jonquils. (Blue Mountain is Mr. Williams' poetic name for Clarksdale, the standard symbol in his plays for romantic, happy youth.) Not having seen her husband growing old and ugly enables her to preserve her romantic image of him. That the father does not appear directly in the play suggests that Tennessee Williams could not view him with sufficient objectivity to portray him. The photograph apparently represents the standard view the outside world caught of the gay [carefree], soldierly C.C. Williams, whom his son hated so much that the sweetness would have gone out of the play if he had been included.

To Tom Wingfield, on the other hand, his father represents escape. He says of him, in the narrator's preface to the story, "He was a telephone man who fell in love with long distances; he gave up his job with the telephone company and skipped the light fantastic out of town." Then follows a hinted admiration of his romantic disappearance: "The last we heard of him was a picture post-card from Mazatlan, on the Pacific coast of Mexico, containing a message of two words—'Hello—Goodbye!' and no address." Tom's interest in his father's wanderlust, at the beginning of the play, prepares us for Tom's departure at its end. The picture itself, an enlarged photograph of Tom's own face, further emphasizes the similarities of their natures. Thus, while the father still personifies love to the romantic memory of the middle-aged Amanda, he symbolizes another kind of romance to his son—the romance of escape and adventure.

Amanda Both Romantic and Practical

In discarding the real father's part, Tennessee Williams found it necessary to endow the mother with some masculine practicality, thus giving Amanda Wingfield an exceedingly complex personality. Like Myra of *Battle of Angels*, she has her past to recall and her present to endure. One had Moon Lake and love in the vineyard, the other Blue Mountain and gentleman callers. Amanda is, obviously, far more the lady, the Southern aristocrat, than the more voluptuous Myra. The only way Amanda can live with ugly reality is to retreat into her memories; there is no sexual solution for her. Her clothes, her speech, and her ideals for her children declare her belief in the past and her rejection of the present. As the author says of Amanda, "She is not paranoiac, but her life is paranoia."

The feature of this woman, which makes her a more admirable character than the later Blanche of *Streetcar* [*A Streetcar Named Desire*] is the anomalous element of practicality encased in her romantic girlishness. Although she has approached much of her life unrealistically, her plans for her children and her understanding of their shortcomings are grimly realistic. Even when refusing to admit it, she knows Laura will never marry. She then tries to find Laura a protective corner of the business world. When this fails, she rallies for the valiant but hopeless attempt to marry the girl off. This second failure, we feel, is less tragic for the daughter than for the mother.

Here we see the quality that Williams suggests from the beginning as the key to her character—her heroism. This, rather than her romantic turn, is her attraction. At the end of the play, when Tom has left, Amanda bends over Laura, huddled upon the sofa, to comfort her. By then, the audience realizes that Amanda herself is in greater need of this sympathy than the quietly resigned Laura. "Now that we cannot hear the mother's speech," says Williams, "her silliness is gone and she has dignity and tragic beauty."

We see this heroism in Amanda in her relations with Tom as well as with the more delicate and more romantic Laura. Although Tom understands the personality of his mother better than any other character in the story, he is more visionary and irresponsible than she is. He cannot see or accept the necessities of their life. Because of this and her previous experience with a romantic husband, she discourages Tom's attempts at a poetic or a nautical career. She returns the D.H. Lawrence novel [that Tom is reading] to the library and nags at him whenever he escapes to a movie. She prods him to take an interest in practical things, like Jim's night classes in electrodynamics. Here, as with her daughter, she is doomed to failure. Consequently, her final line is, "Go, then! Then go to the moon—you selfish dreamer!" Amanda is better able to speak these words with understanding because she shares his yearnings. Her dream has been smashed by reality, but has not been forgotten.

Modernity Is Not Kind to the Wingfields

Tom is a poet who is desperately unhappy in his warehouse job, and, as yet, frustrated in his poetry. Since Tennessee Williams knows something of this not-very-tender trap, he speaks with feeling about the afflictions of the machine age. Believing that many, like himself, are poetic rather than mechanistic, he considers surrender to the machine a perversion of man's nature. His escape, heartless though it may seem, is a "necessary and wholesome measure of self-preservation" (as [critic] John Gassner expresses it).

Laura, like [Williams's sister] Rose, obviously can't escape into movies, alcohol, or literature; she simply isn't that violent or decisive. Her retreat is into a world of glass and music. Her father's old phonograph records provide her with escape that the unfamiliar new tunes can't provide. In the short story out of which the play grew, "Portrait of a Girl in Glass," Tom occasionally brings new records to his sister, but she seldom cares for them because they remind her too much of "the noisy tragedies in Death Valley [her name for the back alley where a dog kills stray cats] or the speed-drills at the business college." Her collection of glass absorbs her time. She spends hours polishing the tiny animals that are as delicate and fragile as she.

Unable to adapt to the modern scene of electro-dynamics, she lives in a world of candlelight and fantasy. The encounter with the machine age is brief and useless. Laura could no more learn to type than Tom could ever come to like his job. Yet, unlike Tom, Laura seems not to feel the ugliness and entombment of their lives. Incapable of his violence, she never steps into the world for fear it would be impossible to bear. She merely stands at the brink and catches what she can of its beauty without becoming a part of it—a lovely picture of the simple Rose, who all through her brother's life has represented to him everything good and beautiful, soft and gentle.

Laura Images Society's Misfits

Laura's early surrender is explained at the opening of the play by an allusion to an illness in childhood which left her crippled, one leg slightly shorter than the other and held in a brace (a physical parallel to Rose's mental affliction). The author explains, "Stemming from this, Laura's separation increases till she is like a piece of her own glass collection, too exquisitely fragile to move from the shelf."

Her mother is both Laura's disease and her brace. It is Amanda's forcefulness that allows Laura to walk at all, but it is also Amanda's example that discourages Laura from walking naturally. At one point, Laura puts on her mother's old coat, which of course is a poor fit for her, an action symbolic of her vague efforts at imitating a personality so alien to her powers and her own nature. She knows that she is like the unicorn or the blue rose, wrong for real life. Laura cannot see that Amanda exaggerates this wrongness by her impossibly romantic dreams. When Laura entered her high-school classes late, the sound of the brace on her leg seemed to her like claps of thunder. She thinks her affliction is dreadful because Amanda thinks it is. This flaw, a symbol of the crippling of a sensitive person thrust into a world unwilling to make allowances for sensitivity, becomes the cause of her separation from reality.

For Tennessee Williams, his sister became a symbol of the sensitive and the outcast, for their sensitivity invariably subjects them to mutilation. It is no accident that Laura's story appears in the collection of early fiction, eventually published under the title *One Arm*. Every important character in the book—the college students, the vagrant poet, the sallow little masochist, the perverted artist, the consumptive factory worker, the one-armed male prostitute, and the girl with her glass menagerie, can be destroyed at a touch. All, like Laura, are crippled in some way. The radiance of such people is like a "piece of translucent glass touched by light, given a momentary radiance, not actual, not lasting."

Scene from a 2007 production of The Glass Menagerie *at the Apollo Theatre in New York City. Because Tom failed to pay the light bill, Laura and Jim, the gentleman caller, must talk by candlelight.* © Geraint Lewis/Alamy.

Jim Represents the Real World

Laura contrasts with the normal, middle-class, realistic Jim, with whom she falls dreamily in love. Their views show their complete diversity. For example, when they discuss her favorite animal, the unicorn, Laura thinks of him as intrinsically different from his companions, while Jim sees him simply as a horse with a horn. In the same way, Jim sees the defect in Laura's leg as only unfortunately incidental to her normal body, while Laura feels that the flaw transforms her whole being. Jim can sympathize with Laura's world of glass and candlelight for this evening, but his real interests are in the modern mechanical world of self-improvement. He is the only character in the play who goes out of the house into a normal world of "reality." Tom emphasizes this in the opening and closing lines of the play; he is an emissary from another world; he does not belong to the Wingfield world of dreams and fears and unexpressed desires.

Jim is not an especially effective character study because Williams can feel little sympathy with such a substantial and placid citizen. Yet he is a kindly reminder of the reasonable, normal human pattern, like the men Williams had met at the shoe factory—clean-living, honest, sweet-natured, materialistic, eager American businessmen. The gently satirical portrait bears no relationship to the later, bitter portraits of C.C. Williams.

Since it is characteristic of Amanda, more than of the others, to long for everything Jim represents, he is for her an archetype of the "long delayed but always expected something we live for." Unintentionally, Jim breaks up the Wingfield dreams. We suspect that his entrance into the household is part of a recurring pattern. Every contact with the real world has shattered Amanda's unrealistic hopes over the years.

The setting of *The Glass Menagerie* was interesting in its symbolism and technical experimentation. Moving from the deep South to St. Louis for his story, Williams retains the memory of the South, as a haunting presence under the superimposed Midwestern setting. The audience, never seeing the gracious mansion that was the scene of Amanda's girlhood, feels its remembered glory and its contrast to the mean present. Awareness of the past is always an element in Williams' plays. His characters live beyond the fleeting moments of the drama—back into a glowing past and shrinking from a terrifying future. For both Amanda and the later Blanche of *Streetcar*, the South forms an image of youth, love, purity, all of the ideals that have crumbled along with the mansions and the family fortunes.

Contemporary Perspectives on Family Dysfunction

Some Parents Are Too Toxic to Tolerate

Richard A. Friedman

Richard A. Friedman is a professor of clinical psychiatry at Cornell Weill Medical College in New York.

Although people tend to think that all parents are loving and nurturing to their children, the sad truth is that there are some perfectly normal people who are cursed with truly awful parents, maintains Friedman in the following article. Whether because of mental illness or a deep-seated personality flaw, some parents form toxic relationships with their children, Friedman explains. In these situations, sometimes the best thing an adult child can do is to sever the relationship with the offending parent, the author contends.

You can divorce an abusive spouse. You can call it quits if your lover mistreats you. But what can you do if the source of your misery is your own parent?

Granted, no parent is perfect. And whining about parental failure, real or not, is practically an American pastime that keeps the therapeutic community dutifully employed.

Some Parents Are Truly Bad

But just as there are ordinary good-enough parents who mysteriously produce a difficult child, there are some decent people who have the misfortune of having a truly toxic parent.

A patient of mine, a lovely woman in her 60s whom I treated for depression, recently asked my advice about how to deal with her aging mother.

"She's always been extremely abusive of me and my siblings," she said, as I recall. "Once, on my birthday, she left me a message wishing that I get a disease. Can you believe it?"

Over the years, she had tried to have a relationship with her mother, but the encounters were always painful and upsetting; her mother remained harshly critical and demeaning.

Whether her mother was mentally ill, just plain mean or both was unclear, but there was no question that my patient had decided long ago that the only way to deal with her mother was to avoid her at all costs.

Now that her mother was approaching death, she was torn about yet another effort at reconciliation. "I feel I should try," my patient told me, "but I know she'll be awful to me."

Should she visit and perhaps forgive her mother, or protect herself and live with a sense of guilt, however unjustified? Tough call, and clearly not mine to make.

Dealing with Toxic Parents

But it did make me wonder about how therapists deal with adult patients who have toxic parents.

The topic gets little, if any, attention in standard textbooks or in the psychiatric literature, perhaps reflecting the common and mistaken notion that adults, unlike children and the elderly, are not vulnerable to such emotional abuse.

All too often, I think, therapists have a bias to salvage relationships, even those that might be harmful to a patient. Instead, it is crucial to be open-minded and to consider whether maintaining the relationship is really healthy and desirable.

Likewise, the assumption that parents are predisposed to love their children unconditionally and protect them from harm is not universally true. I remember one patient, a man in his mid-20s, who came to me for depression and rock-bottom self-esteem.

It didn't take long to find out why. He had recently come out as gay to his devoutly religious parents, who responded by disowning him. It gets worse: at a subsequent family dinner, his father took him aside and told him it would have been better if he, rather than his younger brother, had died in a car accident several years earlier.

Though terribly hurt and angry, this young man still hoped he could get his parents to accept his sexuality and asked me to meet with the three of them.

The session did not go well. The parents insisted that his "lifestyle" was a grave sin, incompatible with their deeply held religious beliefs. When I tried to explain that the scientific consensus was that he had no more choice about his sexual orientation than the color of his eyes, they were unmoved. They simply could not accept him as he was.

I was stunned by their implacable hostility and convinced that they were a psychological menace to my patient. As such, I had to do something I have never contemplated before in treatment.

At the next session I suggested that for his psychological well-being he might consider, at least for now, forgoing a relationship with his parents.

I felt this was a drastic measure, akin to amputating a gangrenous limb to save a patient's life. My patient could not escape all the negative feelings and thoughts about himself that he had internalized from his parents. But at least I could protect him from even more psychological harm.

Easier said than done. He accepted my suggestion with sad resignation, though he did make a few efforts to contact them over the next year. They never responded.

Of course, relationships are rarely all good or bad; even the most abusive parents can sometimes be loving, which is why severing a bond should be a tough, and rare, decision.

Dr. Judith Lewis Herman, a trauma expert who is a clinical professor of psychiatry at Harvard Medical School, said she tried to empower patients to take action to protect themselves without giving direct advice.

"Sometimes we consider a paradoxical intervention and say to a patient, 'I really admire your loyalty to your parents— even at the expense of failing to protect yourself in any way from harm,'" Dr. Herman told me in an interview.

The hope is that patients come to see the psychological cost of a harmful relationship and act to change it.

Eventually, my patient made a full recovery from his depression and started dating, though his parents' absence in his life was never far from his thoughts.

Psychological Damage Can Be Undone

No wonder. Research on early attachment, both in humans and in nonhuman primates, shows that we are hardwired for bonding—even to those who aren't very nice to us.

We also know that although prolonged childhood trauma can be toxic to the brain, adults retain the ability later in life to rewire their brains by new experience, including therapy and psychotropic medication.

For example, prolonged stress can kill cells in the hippocampus, a brain area critical for memory. The good news is that adults are able to grow new neurons in this area in the course of normal development. Also, antidepressants encourage the development of new cells in the hippocampus.

It is no stretch, then, to say that having a toxic parent may be harmful to a child's brain, let alone his feelings. But that damage need not be written in stone.

Of course, we cannot undo history with therapy. But we can help mend brains and minds by removing or reducing stress.

Sometimes, as drastic as it sounds, that means letting go of a toxic parent.

Parents Must Stop Micromanaging Their Children's Lives

Angela Mulholland

Angela Mulholland is a staff writer for CTV News, a division of the CTV Television Network in Canada.

Parents need to reclaim an earlier, less overbearing approach to child rearing, Mulholland explains in the following selection. She reports on the findings of clinical psychologist Alex Russell, who contends that parents engage in far too much meddling in their children's lives and that this constant interference is resulting in a generation of kids that will lack the coping skills needed for adult life. "Helicopter parents" who hover over their children and go to great lengths to protect them from hurt or failure are doing more harm than good, according to Russell.

Parents, it doesn't need to be this hard.

Remember when parenting didn't mean constant nagging, cajoling, bribing and begging? When you could stand back and watch your kids from the sidelines, doing their thing without your help?

It's time for parents to return to those days, and to stop micromanaging every aspect of their children's lives, says clinical psychologist Alex Russell, the author of "Drop the Worry Ball: How to Parent in the Age of Entitlement."

Russell argues in his book that parents have become entirely too wrapped up in their children's lives, worried that if their children aren't successes in the classroom, on the hockey rink, or in the playground, it reflects badly on them.

"More and more parents over-identify with their children's outcomes. How well our kids do feels much more than ever to be a reflection of ourselves," Russell says in a phone interview.

But all this overmeddling is breeding a generation of kids who can't cope without someone telling them what to do and who expect that everything they want to be handed to them.

Helicopter Parents

Many of us already know this, and love to snicker at so-called "helicopter parents." The problem is that oftentimes, those parents who say they are sick of "hoverers" are the very same ones who will chauffeur their children to school, finish their kids' science projects, or chew out their kids' hockey coaches when their child gets cut from the team.

The solution, says Russell, requires not just parents vowing to stop the madness. It also requires a complete cultural shift. And one of the first things that needs to change, he says, is the education system.

"The school-parent-student triangle is way out of whack," he says. "We've got a school system that recruits parents into their children's academic lives from Day 1 and keeps them there."

In his book, Russell and co-author Tim Falconer point to the "agenda books" that are handed out in Toronto schools so that parents can check their children's homework every day and then sign off on it.

The school board's intentions with these books are good, says Russell. Research does show that when parents take an active interest in their children's schoolwork, the kids do better. But the agendas send the message that parents need to be homework police for their children, and that's absurd, says Russell.

That might work in a child's early school years, so that parents can help set the foundation for good study habits, he says. But at some point, they need to let kids figure it out for themselves.

"We want our children to develop their own relationship with school and achievement. And that means that all of us—educators and the kids themselves too—want to get parents out of the equation as soon as possible. We need to wean kids off of their parents. But instead we have policies that do just the opposite."

A Trend Toward Backing Off

The good news is that after years of an education system that was focused on boosting children's self-esteem and avoiding failure, the pendulum has begun to swing back—even in the last five years or so, Russell says.

Parents know they need to back off and allow their kids the chance to make their own mistakes. The problem is they often don't know how to begin. Russell says the key to let go of the worry ball and hand it over to our children so that they can take over their own lives.

A hands-off parenting style doesn't mean sitting back and doing nothing at all, though. It means taking a new approach.

"It's less of the active parenting: the directing, cajoling reminding, threatening, bribing, and instead getting back to the simple 'minding' of your child. That means paying attention, being interested, but not meddling and overreacting," Russell says.

Allowing kids more independence is not easy in a world where children rarely ever stray outside their parents' gaze. And it can be hard to engage in what he calls "benign neglect" in a world that looks down on any parent who would allow their kids to fail an exam if they chose not to study.

In The Glass Menagerie, *Amanda, played here by Laurette Taylor in the original 1945 Broadway production of the play, typifies a type of overbearing parent.* © George Karger/ Time & Life Pictures/Getty Images.

Much of that pressure and shame comes from fellow parents—ironically, often the very same ones who say they can't stand helicopter parents, Russell says. That parental peer pressure can be a powerful force to push against, he says. So, it's likely many of us will feel like bad parents if we let our kids begin to fend more for themselves.

"We have a huge sense of moral obligation to not let our children fail. Some of this is good. It's good that we're more sensitive parents, and that we know more about childhood development and their emotional health. But this level of moral obligation drives us to excessive length, and makes it hard to sit back."

Small Failures Are Helpful

Becoming a hands-off-but-always-there parent is not an easy switch to make. But it's crucial if we want to raise children who become resilient, self-sufficient adults.

"If you're going to step back and let your children take control of something that you've been organizing for him his whole life, it's almost certainly going to get worse before it gets better. You need to be ready for that," he says.

That means following through. When our children do fail, we need to check our response, because the temptation will be to say something like, "See what happens when you . . . ?" or "What you really should have done was . . ."

Kids, like anyone else, tune out of that kind of talk.

"It takes kids' attention off the mistake itself and the solution, and puts it on their nagging parent, who they can then resent," says Russell.

The better approach, he says, is to say something like, "Gosh I'm really sorry to hear about that," then leave it at that and let the child figure out for themselves where they went wrong.

And we should celebrate when our children fail, because it's the key to growth, he says.

"We don't want catastrophic failure, but we should be cheering for some painful, non-catastrophic failure."

Children of Alcoholics Can Learn to Cope

Paula Hunt

Paula Hunt is a writer for Current Health, *a Weekly Reader educational publication for young people.*

One out of every four children and teens in the United States lives with an alcoholic, Hunt reports in the following article. Living with an alcoholic puts tremendous emotional and physical strain on a child, Hunt maintains. Among the risks associated with living in a home where alcohol is abused are becoming an alcoholic oneself, learning and eating disorders, teen pregnancy, and suicide, she explains. It is possible for children to develop coping skills to help them avoid these risks, Hunt suggests, and organizations such as Alateen can be helpful.

Lucy has never appeared in a movie or play, but the 17-year-old feels as if she's had enough acting experience to do both. At school she was the "bad girl" who talked back to teachers and never backed down from a confrontation. At home she acted the part of the "good girl" who always did as her parents asked and never got into trouble.

Playing different roles depending on whom you're with and where you are is common for kids who have an alcoholic in the family. That's the way Lucy coped with living with a father who has the disease. "It was so tiring," says Lucy, who lives near St. Louis.

"It was really stressful [and] scary, and I'd get angry a lot," she explains. "I ended up becoming friends with a girl and hung out with her parents at her house. I stayed there almost

Paula Hunt, "Bottled Up: Family Emotions Go Haywire When Alcoholism Hits Home," *Current Health 2: A Weekly Reader Publication*, vol. 35, no. 6, February 2009, p. 16.

every night." Lucy felt she was the only one with a father who brought along six-packs of beer to nice restaurants, picked on her when he'd had too much alcohol, and seemed to prefer his drinking buddies to his family.

Secrets in Plain Sight

But Lucy isn't alone. Eleven million people under the age of 18 in the United States live with someone who's an alcoholic. That's one of every four kids and teens.

If the problem is so widespread, why don't we know more about it? When it comes to families and alcoholism, there's a code of silence, says Jerry Moe, the national director of children's programs at the Betty Ford Center, a treatment program in Rancho Mirage, Calif. Families deny there's a problem by not discussing it, which makes the problem worse.

Family, Fear, and Side Effects

There is no typical alcoholic family. Some families risk being evicted from their homes and separated, with children taken into government custody. Other families manage to keep up appearances so that from the outside nothing seems to be wrong. In one home there may be physical violence and furniture thrown across the room, while a dark, moody silence pervades another.

The mental and physical health effects are real. Children of alcoholics are at greater risk for eating disorders, learning disorders, teen pregnancy, and suicide. They are more likely to develop alcohol addictions themselves or become romantically involved with alcoholics when they grow up.

But kids and teens react in all kinds of ways to living with an alcoholic. Some have headaches all the time or can't sleep. Some get into trouble at school, while others are overachievers. Some start to drink or abuse drugs, while others are squeaky clean.

There may be depression. Anxiety. Rage. Shame. Guilt. Fear. It's confusing and, as the kids of alcoholics will tell you, totally unfair.

Lucy felt all of those things and sometimes still does, but she's learned to put the feelings in perspective. If her father makes comments about her weight when she's eating potato chips, she doesn't feel hurt the way she used to; instead, Lucy accepts that eating potato chips might not be the healthiest thing—and she can live with that. "I used to blame my dad for how I felt and wish he would change, but now I know that the only thing that I can control is my reactions to what he does," says Lucy.

Crystal's Story

Crystal, 16, also knows what it's like to live with an alcoholic parent. She got help through Alateen, a community-based support program for teens whose lives are emotionally or physically affected by alcoholics. At the meetings, teens learn how they can change their lives for the better, not how they can change their parents' drinking.

Crystal's first Alateen meeting two years ago was the first time she'd talked about her father's drinking—ever. "It was a real gut-spiller, that's for sure," laughs Crystal, who lives in a small town near the Mississippi River. "I'd just held everything in for so long, but being around people who didn't judge me helped a lot."

Talking is something that can help any child of an alcoholic. "Find someone you trust to talk about it with," says Moe. "It could be a friend or a school counselor, a relative, a coach, a minister, a teacher. But being with other kids who've also been embarrassed, who also feel guilty, and who've also felt ashamed or angry is key."

What's also important is realizing that you're not the reason your parent drinks. Teens sometimes think they're to blame for a parent's or loved one's alcoholism. But your behavior, your personality, how you look, or how you act isn't the cause for someone's decision to drink. "My dad stopped drinking for a while, and then he started again, and I used to think it was my fault," says Crystal. "But I know now that his drinking has nothing to do with me."

Help, Hope, and Healing

Alcoholism is a complicated disease that has its roots in a person's genes and his or her environment. Someone unfamiliar with alcoholism might think it's easy to stop drinking, but it's not. Alcoholics have an uncontrollable need to drink that can't be stopped by their own willpower or anyone else's love or pleading. The bottom line: No matter what you do, you can't cure alcoholism.

What has helped Lucy is learning, through Alateen, how to separate her father from his disease so that she doesn't take his behavior personally. She still loves her father, but she hates alcoholism. "You wouldn't blame someone with cancer for being tired, would you?" she says.

But there is hope and, if you're living with an alcoholic, you aren't helpless. "There's always a light at the end of the tunnel," says Rebekah Brown, a social worker in Columbia, Mo. "But first you have to take care of you. Get involved in sports or art or music and express yourself through that. Find something that you love to do and people you can trust to talk to." Opening up about these problems and working through them can be difficult and even painful, but the effort is worth it.

The teens *Current Health* spoke with have learned how to cope with the situation. Crystal's father has stopped drinking and things are better at home. But she reminds herself that even if he starts again, she's not going to blame herself. "I've learned it's his problem, not mine," she says.

Lucy's father still drinks and things aren't great at home. But she no longer feels she has to pretend she's someone else all the time. "I used to not talk very much, but now I don't shut up," says Lucy. "I try not to be so much of a people pleaser, and I try to put myself first." She can finally just be Lucy.

The Absence of a Father Is Linked to Delinquency in Males

Deborah A. Cobb-Clark and Erdal Tekin

Deborah A. Cobb-Clark is on the faculty of business and economics at the Melbourne Institute of Applied Economics and Social Research at the University of Melbourne in Australia. Erdal Tekin is in the Department of Economics at the Andrew Young School of Policy Studies at Georgia State University.

A dramatic increase over the past fifty years in the numbers of families headed by only mothers has caused researchers to examine the role that fathers play in child rearing, according to Cobb-Clark and Tekin in the following paper. An analysis of available data led the researchers to conclude that teenage boys living in a home with no father present were more likely to engage in delinquent behavior than their counterparts in two-parent households. Cobb-Clark and Tekin report that there is no similar pattern for girls—living in a home with no father present does not result in delinquent behavior among females.

Over the past fifty years, modern families have been indelibly altered by dramatic increases in the prevalence of non-marital childbearing, divorce, and remarriage. In the United States, for example, nearly four in ten births are to unmarried women and the fraction of children under age 18 living in mother-only families has risen from 8 percent in 1960 to 23 percent in 2010 [according to the US Census]. Overall, 30 percent of U.S. children are estimated to spend some time

Deborah A. Cobb-Clark and Erdal Tekin, "Fathers and Youth's Delinquent Behavior," *National Bureau of Economic Research Working Paper No. w17507*, October 2011. Copyright © 2011 by the National Bureau of Economic Research. All rights reserved. Reproduced by permission.

living in stepfamilies. This dramatic trend toward father-absent families is similar in most countries around the world and has focused the attention of policy makers and researchers alike on the important role that fathers play in child and adolescent development. For example, the 1996 welfare reform legislation in the United States places significant emphasis on family structure by incorporating family formation and the maintenance of two-parent families as one of its primary components. Most recently, President [Barack] Obama signed into law the Claims Resolution Act of 2010, which authorizes $150 million for programs promoting healthy marriages and responsible fatherhood.

Fathers' Involvement Benefits Children

Previous research has shown that fathers' involvement with their children is linked to higher academic achievement, improved social and emotional well-being, and a lower incidence of delinquency, risk taking, and other problem behaviors. However, it appears to be the quality—rather than the frequency—of fathers' interaction with their children that matters, making it vital to study fathers' relationships with their children in depth.

Much of the early research assessed the role of fathers in two-parent families, leaving many questions about the consequences of living with biological fathers versus stepfathers and the contributions of non-residential fathers unanswered. In the intervening years, non-residential fathers and stepfathers have become the focus of substantial research effort, though the literature on each has developed somewhat separately. Research on stepfathers typically ignores children's relationships with their non-residential fathers, while research on non-residential fathers often does little more than simply account for the fact that mothers may have remarried. Importantly, the handful of studies which do account for the full complexity of children's family relationships paint a much more cautious picture about the positive consequences of fathers' engage-

President Barack Obama signs the Claims Resolution Act of 2010 into law. Included in the law is $150 million dedicated to programs that support healthy marriages and fatherhood. © AP Images/J. Scott Applewhite.

ment with their young and adolescent children. [Researchers A.] Kalil et al. find that living in closer proximity to ones biological father after divorce is associated with poorer outcomes in young adulthood, for example. [A.S. Vogt] Yuan and [H.A.] Hamilton conclude that a close, non-conflictual relationship with stepfathers improves adolescent outcomes, however "involvement with non-residential fathers provides little benefit for adolescents and may even be detrimental." Similarly, economists attempting to unravel the separate effects of family breakdown on young people often conclude that what matters most when fathers leave is not the loss of their presence per se, but rather the loss of their income.

An Assessment of Fathers' Role

Our goal is to contribute to this emerging literature by assessing the impact of biological fathers, both residential and non-residential, and residential stepfathers on the likelihood that youth will engage in a range of delinquent behaviors including property crime, violent crime, selling drugs, taking part in gang fighting, and a composite measure of criminal activity. We allow fathers to influence youths' behavior through (i) the amount of time they spend doing things with and talking to young people; (ii) the contributions they make to household income; and (iii) simply being present in the household. We are particularly interested in the following questions: How does the incidence of delinquent behavior vary across family structures? Does spending time with or talking to fathers reduce the likelihood that youth will engage in delinquent behavior? Finally, does accounting for the extent to which fathers are involved with young people help us to understand the link between youths' delinquent behavior and the types of families they are growing up in?

In addressing these questions, we analyze data from the National Longitudinal Survey of Adolescent Health (Add Health). This data set is ideal for our purposes for a number of reasons. Unlike previous researchers, we exploit the longitudinal nature [a longitudinal study tracks the behavior of a group of individuals over a period of time] of the Add Health data to minimize concerns about reverse causality—i.e., the possibility that delinquent behavior may influence fathers' involvement. Moreover, the information that is available in Add Health about family structure, the nature of fathers' involvement with their children, and household income allows us to simultaneously consider the multiple pathways through which fathers might matter. Detailed data on family background, in particular, mothers' relationships with their children are also important in minimizing the potential for unobserved heterogeneity to confound our estimates. Finally, we consider delinquent behavior both in adolescence and early adulthood.

Delinquency Is Costly to Society

Understanding the link between fathers' involvement with their children and youths' delinquent behavior is critical because the decision to engage in risky or criminal behavior often has substantial social, economic, and health costs for adolescents themselves, their families and society more generally. In 2008, for example, U.S. law enforcement agencies made an estimated 2.11 million arrests of young people under the age of 18, while the Centers for Disease Control (CDC) report that youth violence is the second leading cause of death for young people between the ages of 10 and 24. Designing sensible initiatives to reduce these costs requires fully accounting for the complexity of youths' family relationships and a better understanding of why and how fathers matter.

Fatherless Boys More Delinquent

We find that adolescent boys engage in more delinquent behavior if there is no father figure in their lives. Adolescent girls' behavior is largely independent of the presence (or absence) of their fathers. However, the strong effect of family structure is not explained by the lack of paternal involvement that generally comes with fathers' absence, even though adolescents who spend time doing things with their fathers often have better outcomes. There is also a link between adult delinquent behavior and adolescent family structure that cannot be explained by fathers' involvement with their adolescent sons and is only partially explained by fathers' involvement with their adolescent daughters. Finally, the strong link between adolescent family structure and delinquent behavior is not accounted for by the income differentials associated with fathers' absence. . . .

Adolescent boys who have a father figure in their lives are significantly less likely to engage in subsequent delinquent behavior than are their peers with no father in their lives. For example, the incidence of any form of delinquent behavior is 7.6 percentage points lower among boys living with their biological fathers and is 8.5 percentage points lower among boys who live with stepfathers and have no relationship with their biological fathers. Delinquent behavior is also somewhat less likely among boys with non-residential, biological fathers whether or not their mothers have remarried (4.0 and 5.0 percentage points, respectively), though the former effect is not significant. Fathers are associated with a particularly large reduction in the incidence of violent behavior and gang fighting among adolescent boys. . . .

The presence or absence of father figures, on the other hand, appears to have little relationship with the chances that adolescent girls will engage in delinquent behavior. . . . Overall, adolescent girls living with their biological fathers are 3.6 percentage points less likely than girls with no fathers to engage in some form of delinquent behavior though this difference is not statistically significant.

For Further Discussion

1. How is Tennessee Williams's own experience of growing up in a family where the parents were estranged reflected in his most autobiographical play, *The Glass Menagerie?* What are some similarities between the play and Williams's life? What are some differences? Consult the articles by Gilbert Debusscher and Signi Falk.

2. During childhood, Williams was greatly attached to his sister, Rose. Her mental deterioration and lobotomy were devastating to Williams. What are some of the similarities between Rose and Laura of *The Glass Menagerie?* Consult the selections by John Strother Clayton and Alice Griffin.

3. Amanda is a central figure in *The Glass Menagerie* and her efforts to improve the situations of her children result in one child abandoning the family and the other child retreating further from reality. Critics are divided on whether Amanda is a ridiculous or heroic figure. State your position, considering the essays by Alice Griffin, Roger B. Stein, C.W.E. Bigsby, Eric P. Levy, and Benjamin Nelson.

4. *The Glass Menagerie* is set during the Great Depression, at a time when widespread unemployment shattered the security of many American families. How are the Wingfields impacted by the Depression and how does it affect some of the choices family members make? Consult viewpoints by Roger B. Stein and C.W.E. Bigsby.

5. As of 2010, 23 percent of all children in the United States are growing up in a household without a father present. What are some of the negative impacts that growing up in a home without a father can have on children? Consult the article by Deborah A. Cobb-Clark and Erdal Tekin.

For Further Reading

Edward Albee, *Who's Afraid of Virginia Woolf?*, 1962.

Truman Capote, *Other Voices, Other Rooms*, 1948.

Anton Chekhov, *The Seagull*, 1895.

Hart Crane, *The Bridge*, 1930.

William Faulkner, *The Sound and the Fury*, 1929.

———, *Absalom, Absalom*, 1936.

Lorraine Hansberry, *A Raisin in the Sun*, 1959.

William Inge, *Come Back, Little Sheba*, 1950.

D.H. Lawrence, *Sons and Lovers*, 1913.

Carson McCullers, *The Member of the Wedding: A Novel*, 1946.

Arthur Miller, *Death of a Salesman*, 1949.

———, *The Crucible*, 1952.

Eugene O'Neill, *Long Day's Journey into Night*, 1956.

Tennessee Williams, *A Streetcar Named Desire*, 1947.

———, *Cat on a Hot Tin Roof*, 1955.

———, *Suddenly Last Summer*, 1958.

———, *Memoirs*, 1975.

Bibliography

Books

David M. Allen *How Dysfunctional Families Spur Mental Disorders: A Balanced Approach to Resolve Problems and Reconcile Relationships.* Santa Barbara, CA: Praeger, 2010.

Nina W. Brown *Children of the Self-Absorbed: A Grown-Up's Guide to Getting Over Narcissistic Parents.* Oakland, CA: New Harbinger, 2008.

Albert J. Devlin, ed. *Conversations with Tennessee Williams.* Jackson: University Press of Mississippi, 1986.

Foster Hirsch *A Portrait of the Artist: The Plays of Tennessee Williams.* Port Washington, NY: Kennikat Press, 1979.

Esther Merle Jackson *The Broken World of Tennessee Williams.* Madison: University of Wisconsin Press, 1965.

Richard F. Leavitt, ed. *The World of Tennessee Williams.* New York: G.P. Putnam's Sons, 1978.

Jacqueline O'Connor *Dramatizing Dementia: Madness in the Plays of Tennessee Williams.* Bowling Green, OH: Bowling Green State University Popular Press, 1997.

R.B. Parker	*"The Glass Menagerie": A Collection of Critical Essays.* Englewood Cliffs, NJ: Prentice-Hall, 1983.
Delma E. Presley	*"The Glass Menagerie": An American Memory.* Boston: Twayne, 1990.
Mike Steen	*A Look at Tennessee Williams.* New York: Hawthorn, 1969.
Ralph F. Voss, ed.	*Magical Muse: Millennial Essays on Tennessee Williams.* Tuscaloosa: University of Alabama Press, 2002.
Dakin Williams and Shepherd Mead	*Tennessee Williams: An Intimate Biography.* New York: Arbor House, 1983.
Edwina Dakin Williams	*Remember Me to Tom.* New York: Putnam, 1963.
Tennessee Williams	*Memoirs.* Garden City, NY: Doubleday & Co., 1972.

Periodicals and Internet Sources

K. Balachandran	"Marriage and Family Life in Tennessee Williams," *Notes on Mississippi Writers*, vol. 21, no. 2, 1989.
Mel Gussow	"Tennessee Williams Is Dead at 71," *New York Times*, February 26, 1983.
Allean Hale	"Tennessee Williams's St. Louis Blues," *Mississippi Quarterly*, Fall 1995.

George Hovis
"'Fifty Percent Illusion': The Mask of the Southern Belle in Tennessee Williams's *A Streetcar Named Desire*, *The Glass Menagerie*, and 'Portrait of a Madonna,'" *Tennessee Williams Literary Journal*, Spring 2003.

Elmo Howell
"The Function of Gentlemen Callers: A Note on Tennessee Williams's *The Glass Menagerie*," *Notes on Mississippi Writers*, Winter 1970.

James Lehman
"Rules, Boundaries and Older Children, Part I," *Empowering Parents*, June 2008.

James Lehman
"Rules, Boundaries and Older Children, Part II: In Response to Questions About Adult Children Living at Home," *Empowering Parents*, May 12, 2009.

Lindsay Lyon
"Narcissism Epidemic: Why There Are So Many Narcissists Now," *US News & World Report*, April 21, 2009.

Karyl McBride
"Are You 'Recovering' from the Merry! Merry! and the Ho! Ho! Ho's?," *Psychology Today*, January 5, 2012.

Jeremy Mccarter
"Tennessee Williams Is Back for His Encore," *Newsweek*, March 7, 2011.

Toru Sato
"Codependence Explained in Psychological Terms," *Selfhelp Magazine*, September 8, 2008.

Humaira Tariq   "American Dream and Its Fallibility in Tennessee Williams' *The Glass Menagerie*," *International Journal of Arts and Humanities*, December 31, 2010.

Terry Teachout   "The Irrelevant Masterpiece; the Lessons of the Enduring Success of *The Glass Menagerie*," *Commentary*, June 2010.

So-Young Yoon   "*The Glass Menagerie*: Redeeming the Absent Father," *Journal of Modern British and American Drama*, August 2002.

Index